Beyond the Crossroads

*Traveling Like Christians
on Streets of Faith*

Emmett Diggs

iUniverse, Inc.
Bloomington

Beyond the Crossroads
Traveling Like Christians on Streets of Faith

iUniverse books may be ordered through booksellers or by contacting:

iUniverse
1663 Liberty Drive
Bloomington, IN 47403
www.iuniverse.com
1-800-Authors (1-800-288-4677)

ISBN: 978-1-4759-7734-9 (sc)
ISBN: 978-1-4759-7735-6 (ebk)

Library of Congress Control Number: 2013903360

Printed in the United States of America

iUniverse rev. date: 03/09/2013

Acknowledgments

I would be embarking upon an impossible task if I attempted to recall all who have helped shape my Christian journey, and therefore, have their "thumbprint" on the pages of Beyond the Crossroads. However, there are those whose lives and teachings have significantly influenced my life.

First is the Church. Yes, each of you! I've learned more from you than any other. And you continue to teach me. How? By sharing the depth of your faith. We have been in a pilgrimage together for so long . . . sometimes suffering, sometimes lost, sometimes purposefully, sometimes joyfully . . . but at all times together. Travelling with you has taught me so much. I'm indebted to each of you.

And I've never forgotten the impact of two scholars who significantly influenced my understanding of both the Hebrew and Greek Scriptures of the Bible. Bishop Carlton P. Minnick was my first Bible professor at Ferrum College. Though it has been more than fifty years I still vividly recall being enthralled by his dynamic teaching of the Old Testament traditions. I am certain that my theological understanding of those Old Testament writings is still a reflection of his sharing.

You will find that some of this book centers on the eighth chapter of Mark's gospel. Professor D. Moody Smith, of the Divinity School at Duke University, greatly influenced my understanding of the Gospels. I recall the impact of Mark eight on my life under his profound teaching. The reader will find that influence within the pages of this book.

Beyond the Crossroads would never have been completed without my wonderful wife, Patty, who is my advocate in every endeavor I undertake. Her enrichment of my life's pilgrimage has provided much inspiration for this book.

Finally, I am grateful for Jesus, the Christ, whose presence with me throughout life's pilgrimage has given me direction. Every page is a reflection of His presence and leading.

To my dear wife Patty, who continues to enrich my life with a love beyond any experienced before, and who offers new inspiration as we live the retirement adventure together.

Preface

Since early in my adult life I've been intrigued by the basis of belief in God and why people exhibit certain behavioral patterns. Therefore the pursuit of academic study in the disciplines of theology and psychology moved to the forefront of my endeavors.

After my undergraduate academics I taught psychology and sociology in Florida and then returned to my native Virginia to direct a halfway house for the state. Afterwards, I designed and implemented the Probation House program. The halfway house was a ministry of assisting men transitioning from prison back into society. The Probation House was for teenagers headed for trouble and the program was preventive in nature. The objective was to assist them in turning to more acceptable behavior patterns and to generate a positive self-image.

Later, in answering God's call to full time ministry, I attended Duke University and received a Master of Divinity degree followed by a doctorate in personality development and psychology from

Boston University. This academic background has allowed me a clearer pursuit of God and a greater tolerance and understanding of people. Yet, as you might suspect, a plethora of questions remain for my still questing soul.

During my forty years of Christian ministry I received numerous recognition awards including the Circuit Rider Award in evangelism from the United Methodist Church. Additionally, I received the Community Builder's Award by the Masons of the Commonwealth of Virginia and Volunteer of the Year award from the local Boys and Girls Club. Currently I write pastoral prayers for Prayerideas.org which is an internet ministry. Though retired I am still active in ministry. I teach each Sunday at our church on beautiful Hilton Head Island and am asked to preach occasionally during the Lenten or Advent season. Twice monthly, I offer worship services at an assisted living facility in the community.

As throughout my ministry, I still counsel with many individuals who seek help in their spiritual journeys, marriage difficulties, the loss of loved ones, unemployment and a host of other difficulties that we all face.

This book is offered from an aggregate of the above experiences and hopefully it will enable you as you journey the streets of faith.

Emmett Diggs, Author

Contents

An Introduction

*D*o you know me? Astonishingly, maybe you do. Our predicament is universal. We are an imprisoned people. That very basic "stuff" called skin establishes limits from which there is no earthly parole. There is no way out of one's fleshness; we are prisoners of our very skin!

Maybe it's serving you well now, but soon the years will make a statement and the decaying process will begin. For many of us the statement is being made. The flesh wrinkles and fades, muscles stiffen and retard movement, and the bones become fragile and break. Old age merely makes the prison a shrinking cell.

You and I are confined by more than our skin, though. We are trapped by other more subtle prisons called time, culture, and geography, too. Would you have preferred living during another era of history? But you had no choice. We are prisoners of this age.

Could you have functioned more easily in another culture with different standards by which to live? Have not the mores, folkways, and myths of this culture been the designer and architect of our beliefs and habits? In ways more significant than we want to discover, we are prisoners of society, our environment, the system of thoughts and patterns that surround us daily.

And what if you could have chosen to be born in another land? Would it have been in the Swiss Alps and the mountain grandeur, or near the rolling seas in a tropical land? But you were born here and few of us ever gain the freedom (whether economic or emotional) to change significantly our world's location. We basically stay put, within our own country, in yet another prison called geography.

By now our kinship is affirmed. There are ways in which we need no introduction as our pilgrimages are indeed similar. Our quest for God is no different. We, the creatures, need to make contact with the Creator. The need for a loving, purposeful, social God who has to do with us daily appears cosmic. It will certainly not surprise you to read that peoples of every culture either seek or invent a God to worship. The "still small voice" within the core of the human soul speaks of a helplessness from which we must be delivered, a mystery that compels us to exploration.

Remember how they gathered around Aaron when Moses didn't come back down the mountain soon enough? (Ex.32:1f) "Up" they said to Aaron, "make us gods who shall go before us." And so on command they took off all the gold with which they had adorned themselves, earrings and the like, and gave them to Aaron. He fashioned it "with a graving tool and made a molten calf."

They felt better! "These are our gods, O Israel, who brought us out of the land of Egypt." But it was all a theological scam. They knew better. God is greater than gold.

All of us have known their helplessness—a hollow empty condition of despair. A sense of lostness in the darkness of confusion. The soul whirling as if vertigo had seized it's essence. Looking back across a half century of adult life, I remember most vividly trying to reestablish some semblance of a relationship with God. It had been years since I had prayed. In those days I wanted people to know I didn't need religion, God or the church. In fact, I even "preached a sermon" in a Unitarian Fellowship, poking fun at the faith of which I am now a minister. Perhaps the ego I had needed no God, but the soul within the deep of me cried for a childlike faith. Facing a broken marriage and economic difficulties beyond my ability to cope, suddenly I knew my ego was as fragile as a reed in a nor'easter. In short, I was in desperate need of the God I had so "expertly" denied through smug intellect and shallow wisdom. Many others have travelled on this street called denial.

Everyone's experience is different. For me it took three months of intoxicating work and spiritual agony to feel God's presence again in my life. Still it was by the Lord's grace that we connected finally.

The journey began in a prayer room to the right of the church's foyer entrance. There was a painting of Jesus on the wall over a wooden table with a brass cross in the center. Two candles had been placed strategically on each side of the cross. Cushioned chairs invited me to sit and pray. And then came the shock of my life. I reverently bowed my head in preparation for prayer. I reached out for God but could not pray! I uttered silent and then audible words but they were never heard. No theological debate is needed here. I'm just saying I felt alone and without mercy. That's a good definition of hell! Alone and without mercy. It was a grim experience.

Like the beaten, battered and returning prodigal I hoped for a dance with grace. I knew I didn't deserve grace but the definition of grace is undeserved love! Wasn't I as deserving as that selfish prodigal of Luke 15? Had I not "come to myself" too? (Luke 15:17) Why was I being treated like a stranger in a foreign land? In truth I was a foreigner in a strange land. Long ago that prayer room became such a strange place.

Here some forty years later, I look back on that emptiness. Reflecting, I remember moving back to my native Virginia, spending my lunch hours lying on top of a picnic table looking into the tree tops and the blue sky that domed over the York River. Squirrels scampered and explored the trees, birds sang songs to soothe troubled souls and the gentle breeze reached out to touch even me. It was as if the very hand of the Good Shepherd stretched forth to reclaim a troubled soul. I was glad to be home again.

But there is more in this reflective stage. Now I can see clearly the hand of God weaving a pattern through my often troubled and wounded life. *God has even made good out of the evil I've done!* (Gen.50:20). Like the writers of old I honestly feel compelled to tell you about our God who offers "the way" most clearly through Jesus, the Christ.

Now, here it is. I was not alone. You may be where I was. You may be in a struggle that seems beyond your ability to cope. You are not in that struggle alone either. All of human history has been and is in travail with you. Note throughout the Bible those who struggled with doubts, skepticism, and faith issues, those who struggled with immorality, greed, and a desire for the "gusto" of life. Our journey is grounded in the same vein. I want to affirm that it is all right to be in this gigantic wrestling match with God. Remember Jacob! Read the account offered in Genesis 32:22-32. *But do not struggle alone!* Join hands with the brothers and sisters of the faith who have found their place in the Body of Christ. The church has some honest answers for the troubled who, for whatever reason, journey alone. This book is offered in that spirit.

Now a final compulsion to write this book is to discredit the rubbish. All of this stuff about health and welfare theology is fallacious. Listen to many of today's popular television evangelists. They tell us that God wants you to have a luxury automobile, be rich, dwell in lavish conditions, etc. A huge pile of theological dung. God wants you to have a good heart!

Last time I checked Jesus said, "Do not lay up for yourself treasures on earth, where moth and rust consume . . . but lay up for yourself treasures in heaven . . . for where your treasure is there will be your heart also." (Matt 6:19-21 RSV) Is it not true that you can gain the whole world and lose your own soul? Listen, Jesus tells you not to be anxious about your life, what you'll eat, the clothes you have to wear. Be like the birds of the air and the lilies of the field. God will take care of you. Don't believe that? Then burn this book and your Bible too. Radical? Well, you are either a follower of Jesus or not. We cannot serve two masters. Jesus is tough.

But that is only a partial view. Jesus is also your loving advocate (John 15:14f) and is searching for you and for me. He wants to leave us peace (John 14:7).

Jesus will not leave you the winning lottery ticket . . . just friendship, love and a peace beyond all you've ever experienced. That rich guy in Luke 12: 15f must have received internet scuttle, but Jesus set him straight. "A man's life does not consist of the abundance of his possessions." (RSV) Remember those lilies of the field? Consider them. (Luke 12:27f)

Luke spoke of writing an orderly account of the Gospels. Here I want to offer what seems to me an orderly account for faithing.

"And I applied my mind to know wisdom and to know madness and folly. I perceived that this also is but a striving after wind."
Ecclesiastes 1:17

"For the fate of humans and the fate of animals is the same; as one dies, so dies the other. They all have the same breath, and humans have no advantage over the animals; for all is vanity. All go to one place; all are from the dust, and all turn to dust again. Who knows whether the human spirit goes upward and the spirit of the animals goes downward to the earth?"
Ecclesiastes 3:19-21

New Revised Standard Version

Chapter 1

Is Anybody at the Other End?

t was a hot July morning in 1978. My father, then sixty-two years of age, had just carried a wooden forty-foot ladder from the old paint truck to the shady side of the house. He took pride in his sturdiness as he handled ladders too heavy for his hired help. A few seconds later he fell to the ground. He was the victim of a massive heart attack.

Upon arrival, hours later, at Walter Reed Hospital in Gloucester, Virginia, I felt an uncertainty as I walked to his bed in the coronary care unit. Tubes were protruding from almost every opening in his body, yet he seemed alert and anxious to talk. I was allowed to visit only for a short duration and told him that at the outset. We clasped hands and he shared perhaps the classic statement of his life. "Isn't this something, son, me in here? I thought

I was so damn strong, but we're all just breath and britches." It was a brutal recognition about the human condition, about our fleshness.

"You're right, Dad, you're right," I responded. "We need help from One greater than ourselves." Moments later my father and I, still clasping hands, prayed our first prayer *together*.

I was overwhelmed with so many emotions—his sudden heart attack, the intimacy of our first prayer as father and son, the uncertainty of his future health, and my emerging role as his minister. I remember uttering through the tears, as I left the coronary care area, "Please, dear God, if you're at the other end, help us through this." (Lord, I believe; help thou my unbelief." (Mark 9:24 KJV) That is the fundamental question of life—is there anybody at the other end, or are we facing life alone?

Life does ask certain questions that demand answers. Like the prodigal son of Luke 15, we often come to the "husk times" (Luke 15:16 KJV) of our lives, those times in which we instinctively know we are on a dead-end street and must turn back toward the home port. As I write I know that many are struggling at length on dead-end streets. The problem with the prodigal, and our problem as well, is that we do not see the sign until we've journeyed a long way down that street. Many have spent much of life traveling these streets.

Because we travel so long on the road that ends in "husk times," I am compelled to write this book. It is for all of us who have known, or know, the feeling of despair, who have lived a portion of life and have come up empty. What is being offered here is hope. Not hope in humanity, the multiple sciences, national defense, or living vicariously through children, but a wonderful transcendent hope in a loving God who cares about you and me. We can have hope, not because we can reach up and touch God, but because God is here among us and lifts us above our hopelessness. How often we do not comprehend, or even glimpse, a vision of God's overwhelming grace.

Some years ago I took into the church a wonderfully attractive couple who had a blended family of five children. They searched a long while before they decided to join our church. It was not a matter of procrastination, but rather a decision that required a search for the right worship center. The husband, a well-educated and able man, was called to direct a psychiatric institution in another city. The church was sad when they transferred, for they were so effectively active in our church.

Someone asked him during a Sunday School class how he became so keenly interested in the church. His story, though personal, is a pluralistic story. He thought he would be able to handle life without God, that he really didn't need the church.

As a family unit, he related, they thought they could be self-sufficient. The street of self-sufficiency dead-ends somewhere, and that's where you are . . . . somewhere.

Remember, the prodigal son thought he could be self-sufficient too. We are on the universal dead-end street of life when we feel we can take care of our own lives; captain our own ship, without God. They were not alone in their discovery that the idea of being self-sufficient leads to the "husk times," a street that eventually was marked with a dead-end sign . . . no highway left to travel.

If self-sufficiency street dead-ends with no place left to go, then we find about life that we must turn back and start anew. The relevant question obviously becomes to whom do we turn or return? Is there anybody at the other end?

This question has given pause for preachers to turn time and again to the parable of the prodigal son, for all must return to the loving Father just as the prodigal did. His hope as he ate with the pigs is our hope, also. Flesh must return to the Eternal Other.

As well as the text preaches, it isn't always that simple. I wish it were, for then preaching and counseling would be infinitely more fruitful.

A number of years ago, my wife, Patty, and I would spend week-ends at our home in Mathews, VA. We owned the house but my mother continued to live there. Near bedtime she would begin a conversation about going to bed. Eventually she would say, "Well, if I stay here I'll be here." My mother's name was Ruby so naturally Patty and I called such wisdom a "Rubyism." (I've never been quite sure of the spelling.) We often repeat it with a chuckle. "Well if I stay here I'll be here." She was right. We cannot live afraid to get up, to venture into adventure.

Remember Yogi Berra, the famous Yankee catcher of yesteryear? He once said, "If you come to a fork in the road, take it." Folks laughed. It was one of many famous "yogiisms." We laughed because it seemed obvious, at the fork in the road you have to go one way or the other. *But you don't!* Mouse lemurs hibernate up to seven months a year. Turkish hamsters of the Middle East can hibernate up to ten months a year. Many humans hibernate at crossroads in their lives. How long? Often, for life. We get stuck, paralyzed in the pain and anxiety we feel, afraid to move on . . . frozen at some critical crossroad. Afraid of either path, we hibernate. Many people travel on paralysis street.

Even though we suffer stress staying at the crossroad, we stay there. We call it emotional paralysis. I've been a counselor for many years. The suffering is obvious. Some people just cannot move on. Often we weep for those who choose to stagnate. We were created to see and move beyond the moment.

By the grace of God, not everyone chooses to stay paralyzed. I remember, on June 23, 2011, the powerful testimony of Margaret Lawless, a retired nurse who is enthusiastically active at First Presbyterian Church. It was at a church sports camp with about 15 youngsters present. I was teaching them tennis. She taught them and me much more than tennis. After she got through I said, "Margaret, could you give me a copy of that testimony? I think I have a place for it in my book." You're about to read it now! What a wonderful testimony the kids heard that day! Me too!

"My story is about fear turning into faith. One time I was really afraid. I moved from my home in Iowa, where I grew up and finished college, to prepare for being a nurse. I was assigned to a grand job in a beautiful hospital in Virginia, many miles from my childhood home in Iowa. I had never been near the Atlantic Ocean before. There I was, living in a home with other nurses, and a manager lady who frightened me. She made me feel lonely and unwanted, out of place because I was different from Virginia people. I was discouraged and sad, wishing I could be somebody else. Then I remember God speaking to me. He reminded me of a Bible verse I had learned in a Sunday School class. It was about fear! May I say it for you? 'God does not give us the spirit of fear, but a spirit of power, of love, and a sound mind.' (2 Timothy 1:7 RSV) He gave me new goals.

I felt power because I had faith in Him. I knew the love He poured into my heart made me feel wanted and acceptable. I felt strong in my mind, in the truth of setting the right goals, seeing God bright and clear. I found peace and understanding, feeling thankful no fear could be in me. Are you afraid of anything? How can you throw those fears away? How can you run with courage? You can fix your eyes on Jesus, seeing Him and hearing the plans God has for you. The happy ending to my story about fear of this certain lady was that one day she asked me to listen to her. Guess what?

She told me she had been afraid of me because I came from a place she did not know. She told me she found faith in the very same Bible verse God had given me. God made it possible. Can you believe that! I was so excited I jumped up and let her hug me. The best part of the happy ending to my story is that I met the lady's wonderful son and he became my husband.

I could go ahead without fear, to enjoy power, love, and a sound mind."

Margaret spoke of "love and a sound mind." That's an antithesis of our country's story. Take a look at our national story. We don't journey together very well, do we? Consider politics. "We will not retreat; we will reload." Crosshairs on a map pointing out others with whom we differ politically. All this in a world already prone to violence. Look at our last presidential election. Our president presented as a bozo, a clown, another Hitler, a foreigner without American birthright. Troubled people on angry self-righteous journeys. Looking in the political rear-view mirror, I was in college when they announced the assassination of John F. Kennedy in 1963. Shortly afterwards it was his brother, Robert Kennedy in 1968. Less than twenty years later President Ronald Reagan was shot by John Hinckley. Thankfully, he survived. The obvious is we don't journey well together politically.

I shudder when I rethink the hatred of the bloody civil rights movement of the 1960's. I recall President Kennedy giving a speech on civil rights and the very next day Medgar Evers was shot and killed in his own driveway in June of 1963. And then on April 4, 1968, Dr. Martin Luther King, Jr. was assassinated. America has never replaced him and cannot. In the arena of civil rights we don't journey so well either, do we?

We never seem to learn. Remember recently when Congresswoman Gabrielle Giffords was the victim of that violent assassination attempt by a crazed gunman who succeeded in putting a bullet through her brain causing severe paralysis? I was not impressed when our Congress reluctantly decided they could cross the aisle and sit beside one another to show her respect. Would you have imagined that it would have taken that tragic incident to get our "leaders" to show a little civility? Did I say "leaders?"

And later, with Gabrielle recovering, perhaps faster than we had anticipated, I again was amazed when I turned on the television to hear a current Governor say, "If you are not a Christian then you're not my brother or sister." Did he not hear about religious freedom for all Americans? Maybe I'm writing this book because I'm damn mad. I'm not going to just stand at the crossroad. It's too painful. Not very generative either.

Beyond the tragic secular memories recorded above, I have also been struck by the early religious struggles of the great theologians of our faith; the saints, preachers and philosophers of history. It was never easy for them; why should it be for us?

Perhaps none have stated our dilemma better than the great Danish thought provocator, Soren Kierkegaard. He could find no real link in the Hegelian theme of unbrokenness between the finite and the infinite. For him the world felt foreign, and feelings of hopelessness and abandonment found ample room to reside in his psyche. He expressed it best in his book called *Repetition* (1843):

> One sticks one's finger into the soil to tell
> by the smell in what land one is: I stick my

finger into existence—it smells of nothing. Where am I? How came I here? What is this thing called the world? What does the world mean? Who is it that has lured me into the thing, and now leaves me there? . . . How did I come into the world? Why was I not consulted, why not made acquainted with its manners and customs, but was thrust into the ranks as though I had been bought of a "soul-seller"? How did I obtain an interest in this big enterprise they call eternity? Why should I have an interest in it? Is it not a voluntary concern? And if I am compelled to take part in it, where is the director? 2

That's the question. Where is the Director? I remember when I was a teenager, sitting on a wharf with my life long buddy in Mathews, Virginia where I grew up. I wasn't very religious; in fact, I seldom went to church at the time. Somehow, though, we got into a deep discussion about God and the universe we were experiencing.

Both of us were gazing up into a sea of stars, and at the same time the waters of the Chesapeake Bay were lapping beneath us. The Bay's gentle summer breeze only added to life's wonderful mysteries. We wondered what God was like, supposed God's power to be awesome, and concluded that it was good that

God cared about creation, even about us! I wish that it could have stayed there theologically for me. In that little farming and fishing village everybody believed in God and nobody questioned the Creator's whereabouts.

With continued education, adult experiences, and a greater cognizance of the world in which I lived, I grew skeptical. As I stuck my finger into the "soil" of life, I began to feel more alone. Kierkegaard's questions became my questions. How do I fit in? Why was I born Caucasian? Who decided this to be my time in history? What if I had been born in Russia and not in America? Who chose my parents? Nobody consulted me! What can I find out about life? Is anybody at the other end?

It's been a life-long pilgrimage for me. Why am I here? Does the universe have a purpose? Is there a purposeful Creator who created us with a vocation in mind?

Sure there are folks all around who glibly say "there is a God." I want to ask them, "really?" Who told you? Have you seen God? Where? Are you sure, absolutely sure that God is or are you just a part of "herd" thinking? Thinking what everybody else is thinking. Acknowledge what we seldom admit . . . what you share is your faith . . . different than fact.

We really do want to know the purpose of the universe. It's tantamount. It is not enough to know who created this universe. We'd like to know the

Creator. Would you like to ask God why creation happened? What was the thought behind the plan? But we have no answers. Who has seen, touched or heard the voice of God? Faithing is hard if it's done honestly. I am both scientific and religious. I seek faith and facts. I want my faith to be compatible with logic, or at least with what appears logical to me. We'd be something less than logical if we did not admit that at such depths we struggle. Perhaps this is why, in 1941, Einstein said "science without religion is lame and religion without science is blind."2 (Einstein's God p.22)

But on the other hand it might be worth wondering if faith is not more important than fact. If affirmation is not more substantial than continued searching, even floundering at times in one's religious experience! Exploring mystery is like a rainbow arching the sky. Every rainbow stops our advance, arrests us at the point of first glimpse. Science explains rainbows factually. Yet the mystery and beauty of its colors awakens a deep meaning. We want to get at the substratum of events and causes. We observe lightning, sunrises, erosion of rocks, water freezing and have scientific explanations for each. But what is at the root of the causes? Mystery stands at the cradle of truth. If one cannot get excited about the mystery of the unknown, doesn't want to penetrate beyondness, then that's like being a "snuffed out candle."2 (Einstein's God p.23)

A raging battle exists about creation. What shall we teach our children about creation? Should we teach God's seven day schedule or the scientific Big Bang theory? Certainly we don't want to limit God's creative options through finite thinking. But when I look at the basic two creation stories of Genesis I am struck by those old faithers peeking into the possibilities of such a great mystery. They, like us, wanted answers to "why," what about my place here, and in what direction to go in the journey of living.

James Weldon Johnson (1871-1938), one of the first to break through the barriers of hateful segregation, with brilliant spiritual imagination, pulled back the curtain of mystery and peeked behind to see God framing creation. He was deeply connected with the Eternal One when he shared the following account of creation. Is it accurate? As much as any offering I've ever read. He combines the Genesis accounts with his rich imaginative mind in partnership with the Holy Spirit to offer a teleological God shaping all that we experience as we live each day. You must absorb each word.

> And God stepped out on space,
> And he looked around and said:
> I'm lonely—
> I'll make me a world.
>
> And far as the eye of God could see

Darkness covered everything,
Blacker than a hundred midnights
Down in a cypress swamp.
Then God smiled,
And the light broke,
And the darkness rolled up on one side,
And the light stood shining on the other,
And God said: That's good!

Then God reached out and took the light
    in his hands,
And God rolled the light around in his
    hands
Until he made the sun;
And he set the sun a-blazing in the
    heavens.
And the light that was left from making
    the sun
God gathered it up in a shining ball
And flung it against the darkness,
Spangling the night with the moon and
    stars.
Then down between
The darkness and the light
He hurled the world;
And God said: That's good!

Then God himself stepped down—
And the sun was on his right hand,

And the moon was on his left;
The stars were clustered about his head,
And the earth was under his feet.
And God walked, and where he trod
His footsteps hollowed the valleys out
And bulged the mountains up.

Then he stopped and looked and saw
That the earth was hot and barren
So God stepped over to the edge of the
        world
And he spat out the seven seas—
He batted his eyes, and the lightnings
        flashed—
He clapped his hands, and the thunders
        rolled—
And the waters above the earth came
        down,
The cooling waters came down.
Then the green grass sprouted,
And the little red flowers blossomed,
The pine tree pointed his finger to the sky,
And the oak spread out his arms,
The lakes cuddled down in the hollows of
        the ground,
And the rivers ran down to the sea;
And God smiled again,
And the rainbow appeared,
And curled itself around his shoulder.

Then God raised his arm and he waved his
    hand
Over the sea and over the land,
And he said: Bring forth! Bring forth!
And quicker than God could drop his
    hand,
Fishes and fowls
And beasts and birds
Swam the rivers and the seas,
Roamed the forests and the woods,
And split the air with their wings.
And God said: That's good!

Then God walked around,
And God looked around
On all that he had made.
He looked at the sun,
And he looked at his moon,
And he looked at his little stars;
He looked on his world
With all its living things,
And God said: I'm lonely still.

Then God sat down—
On the side of a hill where he could think;
By a deep, wide river he sat down;
With his head in his hands,
God thought and thought,
Till he thought: I'll make me a man!

Up from the bed of the river
God scooped the clay;
And by the bank of the river
He kneeled him down;
And there the great God Almighty
Who lit the sun and fixed it in the sky,
Who flung the stars to the most far corner
of the night,
Who rounded the earth in the middle of
his hand:
This Great God,
Like a mammy bending over her baby,
Kneeled down in the dust
Toiling over a lump of clay
Till he shaped it in his own image;
Then into it he blew the breath of life,
And man became a living soul.
Amen. Amen. 3

How can we not love the poetic imagination expressed in such magnificent language. Yet, even as poetry it points out that we are here in the middle of an unfinished story. We want to know where it finishes . . . have a conclusion. But all we know is we are part of a colossal story. To whom do we turn for a resolution? I introduced this opening chapter with excerpts from Ecclesiastes, for that writer found God's ways impossible to comprehend. For him after careful observation of the ebb and flow of his time, life had little meaning. He tried living with purpose and then living wantonly and ended up saying, "all is vanity and chasing after the wind." (Ecclesiastes 1:14 NRSV)

Some time ago someone created a cartoon about two fleas, agnostic fleas they were. Both standing in a forest of fur on a dog's back, one says to the other, "Sometimes I wonder if there really is a dog." Well, they wanted to know the truth and they were standing in it—and on it and surrounded by it.

Now there were church fleas everywhere that told them about the dog. The dog can be just about any color and wags its tail because it loves everybody. But the dog will growl if you make it angry. There are always folks who want to tell us about the dog.

The two agnostic fleas represent us all. We don't want to know about the dog, we want to know the dog. And remember this . . . dog spelled backwards is God! Too heavy!

Well, in truth, the church fleas were doing the best they could. They told the two agnostic fleas all they knew about a dog. Just like so many of the church they did not mention their own relationship with this dog. They never mentioned how much this dog meant to them.

What's more important than sharing what the dog (God) means to us in our living of these days? Why is it that we cannot share spiritually together? Often people come to my office simply knowing life is empty, meaningless, without direction, fulfillment or purpose. They are not questing for anything in particular; they just know something is wrong. It is as if people are saying "teach me," but they do not know what they want to learn.

There is even confusion about the difference between being taught and learning. Ultimately the pilgrimage to God is never accomplished through "being taught" by someone else. We must learn individually how to be in relationship with God.

If you do not know Jesus Christ, if your life really does feel empty, fragile and without direction, then you must begin now to change your life's course. Developing proper spiritual habits is a must, for we do not live in a world conducive to real faith growth. There is no minister, guru, psychotherapist, or friend to whom you can go to get your broken world "fixed." In short, you must become so dissatisfied with your present emptiness that you are determined to seek the way of Christ. Spiritual pilgrimages are conceived out of such pain.

Is anybody at the other end presupposes we are at this end. Further, it is from this end that our spiritual journey must begin.

The concern that we mortals should consider is this. Are we among those not seeking what is beyond us? So often people say, "I'm just not inclined to spend time questing for God. That's just not important to me." They create a small world and make a gigantic mistake. The Creator did not create us to abandon faith and not to consider our spirituality. You are here and that's a gift worth your searching for answers and expressing your gratitude. Embrace this moment as it is connected to the eternal always.

There are worldly hurdles that you must ascend if your spiritual journey is to be successful. In a later chapter we will explore these issues in greater detail; however, there are some traps not of your own making. This is a world that can best be described with adjectives such as busy, noisy, impersonal and complex. These are not conditions best suited for one to establish or reestablish a relationship with the Lord. Yet you must learn how to communicate from where you are. Don't be alarmed if you need help with that.

I am reminded of a delightful moment of revelation that came my way out of an experience with my son many years ago. I do not recall how old he was, but he was young enough to be riding a tricycle. I had just bought him a horn and mounted it on the handle bars of the little red tricycle. The horn had a rubber-type balloon on the end closest to him and, if he squeezed that rubber end, it would cause the horn to blow.

I said to Brian, "Son, blow your horn." He immediately bent over, pursed his lips, and blew on his horn as if he were blowing out birthday candles!

The word blow meant something totally different to him than what I intended. He did not know enough about the language. We were not on the same tract.

It was a great lesson in communication. It's a complicated matter to communicate with others who have limited or different experiences than ourselves. I'm convinced that communicating with God evokes emotions and experiences that are often new to us, also. I would encourage you to read the Bible, learn the language of the prophets, of the wisdom writers, and of the Gospels. Seek books of spiritual quality and scholarship that can help in this complicated process. It can only enable your beginning a journey with your Creator. Seek the quiet place with enough time to rid yourself of a hurried feeling. Establish a spiritual language and time with God. God often speaks most clearly when all else is silent. Sometimes silence is the best spiritual language spoken.

A second worldly hurdle that stymies the spiritual journey is the need for security. Long ago there was a slogan circulating that shared "The one who dies with the most toys wins." The truth of that statement, in terms of how we live secularly, exploded in my mind. *We live as if that slogan were true!*

Upon study, one learns that the great spiritual giants of history somehow escaped the almost universal need to gather the "toys" of life. They discovered that a true pilgrimage with God has little to do with developing bases of security and protection against the world. Their security is found within their pilgrimage and relationship with the Lord of life.

Perhaps you've read something of the life of St. Francis of Assisi (1181-1226). An Italian Catholic Friar and preacher who founded the men's Franciscan Order and the women's Order of St. Clare, he is one of the most venerable religious figures in history.

He was the son of a cloth merchant in Assisi and lived the high life typical of a wealthy young man. While going off to war in 1204 A.D. Francis had a vision that turned his life around completely. *He lost his taste for the worldly life.* Instead he begged with the beggars at St. Peter's. That experience moved him to live in poverty. He married his "lady poverty" and spent much of his time asking for God's enlightenment.

Poverty became so central to his character that he felt that absolute and corporate poverty was the essential lifestyle for those members of his Order.

He nursed lepers, gave away his garments and possessions and became a street beggar and preacher. Now, drink deep of this cup. He believed that nature itself was the mirror of God and called all creatures his brothers and sisters. He even preached to the birds! Every day birds eat from my hands and I feel a kinship with St. Francis that has travelled across the centuries. Every bird that lights on my hand is a reflective mirror of our Maker. I see something of the Eternal in each of them as they sing from my hand! (See picture of me and "yellow boy" on the book's back cover).

Compare St. Francis with the rich ruler of Luke 18: 1-25 (RSV). That fellow never sought the mirror of God. He sought security for himself. He was born rich and at the controls; yet there was an emptiness. Like many of that day and this, he went to Jesus. "What shall I do to inherit eternal life?" (Luke 18:18b RSV) After a short time of discussion, Jesus informs him, "One thing you still lack. Sell all that you have and distribute to the poor, and you will have treasure in heaven; and come follow me." (Luke 18:22 RSV)

The scripture relates that he became very sad and went away. He gave up the spiritual journey because he couldn't let go of the "toys." Somehow in the confusion of his day he believed "the one with the most toys wins." Over and over the One sent to us from God reminded those who assembled around Him against gathering "toys" for security. "Sell your possessions, and give alms; provide yourselves with purses that do not grow old, with a treasure in the heavens that does not fail, where no thief approaches and no moth destroys. For where your treasure is, there will your heart be also." (Luke 12:33-34 RSV)

Security might be the twenty first century's most elusive commodity; yet the wisdom of our

Lord remains the same. If you want to really find yourself, seek a cause greater than "toy collecting" for salvation.

Is anybody at the other end? Yes, a thousand times let's affirm the glorious presence of a loving, compassionate God who strides the pathways of our journeys even when we are not aware of the Spirit's presence. A good example of such a silent presence was one Christmas Eve with a full agenda of holiness and excitement planned. The program planned was singing old and familiar hymns with families being together for the first time since last year's Christmas Eve service, communion by intinction, and at the end of the service every person holding a lighted candle in their hands; taking the light of Christ out into the world! What could go wrong? The agenda was so carefully planned.

Well, all went as planned until the soft white cloth was piously lifted from the from the chalice of grape juice. Peering into the juice I was horrified to find two flies "consummating something" within the chalice of juice. More than two hundred people were waiting to be served within the walls of that small church. What would we do now?

I began to feel perspiration popping out on my forehead, and beneath my robe sweat was rolling down my chest. How will I handle this tastefully and in a cryptic fashion? One of the communion stewards wanted to simply scoop the two "lovers" out of the juice but I knew that we had to find another way. I instructed the steward to go wash out the chalice, refill it with fresh juice looking all the while as if it were some holy ritual. I filled the vacant time with words of what a privilege it was to share with the Master. Moisture was still crisscrossing my face and underneath my robe the rolling sweat seemed especially active. I felt like a rendition of Niagara Falls but remained pious until the new juice arrived and was sanctimoniously placed on the Lord's table. We then proceeded to serve.

Afterwards several people shared that this was the most holy Christmas Eve they had ever experienced. "Praise the Lord" I responded with a soaked dress shirt under my robe. God works in strange and mysterious ways. Sometime later I shared the whole experience with the Administrative Board. They thought I ought to write a book about this experience. You just read it!

I hear a voice I had not known;
"I relieved your shoulder of the burden;
your hands were freed from the basket.
In distress you called, and
I delivered you;
I answered you in the secret
place of thunder;
I tested you at the waters of Meribah.
Hear, O my people, while I admonish you!
O Israel, If you would but listen to me!
There shall be no strange god among you,
You shall not bow down to a foreign god.

I am the Lord your God,
who brought you out of the land of Egypt.
Open your mouth wide, and I will fill it.

"But my people did not listen to my voice;
Israel would have none of me.
So I gave them over to their
stubborn hearts,
to follow their own counsels.
O that my people would listen to me,
That Israel would walk in my ways!"
Psalm 81:6-13

Revised Standard Version

Chapter 2

God Has To Do With Us

id you ever study the Adam and Eve story in Genesis 3? There may be more to this ancient sage than we suspect. There is. Our fleshness is in it. Picture if you can, everything being perfect. God is in this holy place, this lush garden, with you. The Creator shows you around, offering you freely, all of creation except for the fruit of one lousy tree! Anyone could have stayed away. Could you ?

Watch out, Eve, there's a snake in the grass! "Psst, Eve, did God say you couldn't eat of that fruit?" Eve is taken back. How did that snake know what was on her mind? She felt vulnerable now at her apparent transparency. "Not only can I not eat it, I cannot even look at it."

We so often overstate when we feel vulnerable. God never said she couldn't look at the fruit, but she would have been better off had she not looked, for you know how it is. The fruit was a delight to her eyes. Sin is of that nature. It most always appears to be a delight. You don't believe that? Then why do we so often eat of the fruit, do it our way instead of God's? Sin *does* appear enticing, delightful, inviting. Let's have some of that fruit. Besides, the serpent is right.

Can't you hear the snake in the hidden places of your soul? You eat that if you want. You be in control of your life. You're wise enough, old enough, and you certainly want to experience life—all of it! Yes, all of it. She's on vulnerability street now. Eve begins to eat—do it her way. But something was wrong. She was alone. When we are uncertain of our actions, we always want somebody else on board with us. Sinning is always easier when we do it together. "ADAM," she called out. He came and they ate! We're all just flesh.

And then it happens. Judgment comes like an undetected tsunami wave. God is everywhere, inescapable. "Adam, where are you?" (Gen. 3:9 RSV)

Quick, Adam and Eve, cover yourselves . . . hide . . . afraid . . . guilty . . . just human after all. Ah, this story is about us. Flesh is weak. We are not God. Our name is Vulnerable.

Listen to the rest of the story. "Adam, why did you eat of the fruit?"

"The woman whom thou gavest me, she gave me the fruit." (Genesis 3:12 RSV) Adam blames it on Eve, and to solidify his position he reminds God that she is the Lord's creation to boot! God turns toward Eve. "The serpent beguiled me," (Gen. 3:13 RSV) she blurts out. The truth leaps out at us! Here it is! We like to drag others in on our sins.

I remember the old school days. Mom asked me, "Why did you do so badly in science, Son?" I said, "The teacher failed most of the class, Mom." There were other variation like "the teacher just doesn't like me." They all had the same design, to drag the teacher in on my failure. Adam and Eve represent us. We are as they were. We call it original sin in theology. That's a heavy load for Adam and Eve to carry. Maybe we ought to get a grip on our role in this history of human sin.

The snake? Her name is Choice. I named her that a few years ago in a sermon. Life is about choosing rights and wrongs, to play god or to let God be God.

There is another important point about this ancient but timeless scripture that is often overlooked. The Lord God of Genesis 3 is a social God. The Lord has to do with us as we live our lives.

Is anybody at the other end? From the beginning the Bible assures us that God cares and is involved in our daily lives, but we continue to live as if God is not. What change would come about if we were in touch, open to the works of the Holy Spirit? The point is that though Genesis 3 proclaims a social, active God in the life of humanity, we often fail to respond. We may never feel God's presence if we never allow the Lord to be present. Tragedy is the name of this street!

If Genesis 3 is a statement about a God who is social and relational (that is who interacts with us), then it becomes imperative that we investigate what and how our relationship forms. With what kind of God are we in relationship? How does God respond to us when we are good (obedient) or bad (disobedient)? Does God give advice, offer guidance, or somehow show us the way? Who is this One on whom ministers say they depend for inspiration? Have you ever been alone with the Alone?

One of the first factors that emerges for us in figuring out who this "relational" God is in our lives is that God does not fit well with the past images of the Eternal One pressed into our brains by all sorts of Sunday School literature and surface conversation. That God was rather like Superman, always arriving just in the nick of time to scatter the evil forces and save the innocent. It's very difficult to get on base with that God in the midst of the tragedies surrounding us. That, no doubt, made it easier for many to leave the church for years. Listen, if God is both all-loving and all-powerful as we too often have been taught, then why is there so much suffering in the world? Why do people starve, freeze and die of terrible terminal diseases?

As children, and many times since, we have listened to the myths of people about how God is.

Too often we make God as we would be pleased for the Lord to be. Recently a parishioner shared one of our golden myths. She had just lost her husband and was feeling the terrible pangs of that emptiness. Mustering up her faith, she looked squarely at me and said, "But God won't put more on us than we can stand."

My mind raced to an event of just a few years ago in a nearby town. There a man was watching his wife die and could "stand" it no longer. He walked to the end of a pier, took off his glasses, removed his false teeth, and stepped off the pier to purposefully drown. He was successful in his endeavor. What would the parishioner say about that man's God? The point is not that God placed a burden on either the woman or the man just mentioned, but that we too often attribute to God characteristics that do not describe God as much as they point toward how we hope God is. Mythology is the name of this street. The question may be, did God make us in God's image, or have we made God in our image?

How about one more of our "golden oldies" from the Old Testament? So many people, churched and unchurched, somehow still hold fast to the basic teachings of Deuteronomy. Perhaps the best summary of that is found in the twenty-eighth chapter where the author states plainly that if you obey God and keep the Lord's commandments, then God will bless you. (Deuteronomy 28:1-14 NRSV)

If you will only obey the Lord your God, by diligently observing all his commandments that I am commanding you today, the Lord your God will set you up high above all the nations of the earth; all these blessings shall come upon you and overtake you, if you obey the Lord your God: Blessed shall you be in the city, and blessed shall you be in the field. Blessed shall be the fruit of your womb, the fruit of your livestock, both the increase of your cattle and the issue of your flock. Blessed shall be your basket and your kneading bowl. Blessed shall you be when you come in, and blessed shall you be when you go out. The Lord will cause your enemies who rise against you to be defeated before you; they shall come out against you one way, and flee before you seven ways. The Lord will command the blessing upon you in your barns, and in all that you undertake; he will bless you in the land that the Lord your God is giving you. The Lord will establish you as his holy people, as he has sworn to you, if you keep the commandments of the Lord your God and walk in his ways. All the peoples of the earth shall see that you are called by the name of the Lord, and they shall be afraid of you. The Lord will make you abound in prosperity, in the fruit of your womb, in the fruit of your livestock, and in the fruit of your ground in the land the Lord swore to your ancestors to give you. The Lord will open for you his rich storehouse, the heavens, to give the rain of your land in its season and to bless all your undertakings. You will lend to many nations, but you will not borrow. The Lord will make you the head, and not the tail; you shall be only at the top, and not at the bottom—if you obey the commandments of the Lord your God, which I am commanding you today, by diligently observing them, and if you do not turn aside from any of the words that I am commanding you today, either to the right or to the left, following other gods to serve them.

The opposite, disobedience to God's commands brings certain catastrophe from God. (Deuteronomy 28:15-24 NRSV)

But if you will not obey the Lord your God by diligently observing all his commandments and decrees, which I am commanding you today, then all these curses shall come upon you and overtake you: Cursed shall you be in the city, and cursed shall you be in the field. Cursed shall be your basket and your kneading bowl. Cursed shall be the fruit of your womb, the fruit of your ground, the increase of your cattle and the issue of your flock. Cursed shall you be when you come in, and cursed shall you be when you go out. The Lord will send upon you disaster, panic, and frustration in everything you attempt to do, until you are destroyed and perish quickly, on account of the evil of your deeds, because you have forsaken me. The Lord will make the pestilence cling to you until it has consumed you off the land that you are entering to possess. The Lord will afflict you with consumption, fever, inflammation, with fiery heart and drought, and with blight and mildew; they shall pursue you until you perish. The sky over your head shall be bronze, and the earth under you iron. The Lord will change the rain of your land into powder, and only dust shall come down upon you from the sky until you are destroyed.

As a clergyman, it is sometimes agonizing to watch people attempt to control God through their own behavior. It is as if they are confident that their attempts at goodness will force from God the blessings of life. They put a hammer lock on God and force God to respond favorably to them. See God, I've been good, now you bless me. With all due respect for their interpretation of the Deuteronomist, we can be certain that this is not the God with whom we are in relationship.

Why such certainty? First, because life's experiences teach us a vastly different lesson. Let's face it, all of us have watched some of the best of our sisters and brothers suffer one tragedy after another. We have known wonderful people who have been raped, others burned alive in the blaze of their own home, and still others innocently butchered and murdered. And all the while some of the most wretched of people are flourishing in their cruelty, hatred and dishonesty toward others.

How does the God of the Deuteronomist fit into all of this, and how do the many modern-day Deuteronomists fit all of this into their mythological theology?

The best reason for not assuming the view of the Deuteronomist is that Jesus Christ taught us differently. A careful reading of Matthew's eschatological Sermon on the Mount offers Jesus teaching that the very nature of God is to treat everyone alike. That very nature of God, who lets the "sun rise on the evil and on the good, and sends rain on the just and on the unjust," is what calls us to love our enemies and pray for those who persecute us. (Matthew 5:44 RSV) Jesus was no Deuteronomist! He shared with us a God of grace, and not a God of retribution!

In short, the heart of the sermon at this point is we are to extend love to our enemies and persecutors because that is the essence of God! Whereas the Deuteronomist teaches about a revealed order that ought to elicit our good behavior (the covenant), Jesus teaches about the very character of God to love us all and to treat us equally despite our choices.

We come up short if we investigate only how God is not. The intent here is to talk about how God is and how God relates to us. Years ago, when I directed a probation house in Williamsburg, Virginia, for troubled youngsters already amiss of the law, I inherited a very special case. He was black, fifteen years old, and physically quite a handsome fellow. Probably he was our most social and likeable resident.

We had set aside one evening a week for group sessions in which one of the residents would be analyzed by his peers. This night we chose to talk about James, the above-described youngster. When he was singled out, he went into a rage quite uncharacteristic of him. He began yelling obscenities, telling us where he was going to kick us, and stating that nobody was going to say anything about him. I knew why he was so hysterical. He was afraid that his peers might find out, through sharing, that he could neither read, write, nor do simple arithmetic. It was his secret of embarrassment for no one else to discover. During the course of the evening his peers unraveled the mystery of his rage and to his surprise, offered him support and understanding. Arrangements were made for James to be tutored, and he was beginning to make strides in areas where he felt so ignorant and embarrassed. Much too quickly he was released from our program and was back on the streets. Why? The rule was you were only allowed into the program for three months. His time was up.

I do not know the whole story, but months later he was arrested for being an accomplice in a murder case. With characteristic succinctness someone said, "They ought to give him life." More emotional than normal, I responded, "Yes, give him life, give him life; give him life because that's something he never had." It was a play on words, but my message was clearly received. He had never experienced the normal opportunities of life.

How is God? If there is anything that we can believe about God, it is that the Eternal One has given us life. An analysis of that "given life" is important in developing a healthy relationship with

God. In a recent confirmation class a ten-year-old girl stated that she thought God created us so God wouldn't be lonely. We cannot be sure, but she may be partially right. That a lonely God would create us makes sense to me. That God would create for the purpose of having meaningful relationships with us furthers the logic. God is not out there or away from us in the Christian perspective. Like Jesus, God is in our midst.

Robert Browning wrote poetically in "Pippa's Song." A partial rendering is as follows.

> The year's at the Spring
> And day's at the morn;
> Morning's at seven;
> And the hillside's dew-pearl'd;
> The lark's on the wing;
> The snail's on the thorn;
> God's in His heaven—
> All's right with the world!

The poetry is superior but the theology needs further thought. In our thinking about God perhaps we ought to leave behind such heavenly language. For me God is no longer residing high above in "His heaven." The Bible speaks of a God who is in our midst like a "burning bush" (Ex.3:3f RSV) or a nocturnal "stranger" wrestling with Jacob throughout the night. (Gen 32:24) God is here and participating in our dilemmas in the Old Testament. In the New Testament incarnation, Jesus is defined as God with skin on and with us as we struggle with our issues. Matthew 18:20 (RSV) tells us that "where two or three are gathered in my name, there am I in the midst of them." Translate that like this . . . two or three sincere folks are assured of Christ's presence and God's answer to prayer.

Paul Tillich writes not of the "height" of God but the "depth" of God! Let's be clear about what these words mean. By "height" Tillich was referring to the God thought of as heavenly and above us. God resides and operates from some place above us in the heavens. By the "depth" of God the meaning is, God is here with us as we struggle. It is here, at the depth of our lives, in all our trials, tribulations and difficulties that we can find God to be nearest. Otherwise would God even be relevant? Would there have been an Exodus or a Cross; that is freedom from slavery in Egypt and from our sinful nature through the cross without a God of "depth"?

We must think that the ultimate truth about God is deep and profound. So why not speak of the depth of God instead of some God high in the sky in a state of beyondness? (Tillich; The Shaking of the Foundations, p 60)4

Like Jesus, God is in our midst. The whole biblical message is about a God who is both present and deeply involved in our lives. Therefore, when we say God has given us life, it is meant in a relational context. We are not just placed here to survive by our own secular efforts, but the "given life" includes our knowledge of an offered relationship with our Maker. That coincides with the scripture for scripturally to be apart from God is death, not life. So God and humanity are in relationship. The Genesis account of creation emphasizes life in this manner.

How is God? As you pilgrimage it is important to understand that God, by God's own choosing, is no longer all-powerful. This does not mean that God is not in charge of the ultimate culmination of history for surely God controls history's destiny, the end times. The focus here is of losing power because God chooses to give us freedom. Recall again that rich third chapter of Genesis. Note that Eve has the freedom to choose and, when she calls Adam to the scene, he also has the same freedom. They can make choices contrary to the will of God because God chose to give them and us freedom to make our own decisions. The simple truth is that when God chose to give humanity the dignity of choosing God let loose of considerable power. Let me explain.

Perhaps recently you have lost a significant amount of parental power and control. It was by your own choosing, but nevertheless you no longer had the same trump cards you once had. You know how you lost power? You reached in your pocket, pulled out the car keys and handed them over to your son or daughter. Once you decided to do that you began to experience something of what God has endured ever since God gave Adam and Eve the keys of freedom to roam the beautiful garden.

Once, you took your children to their destination; now they drive themselves. You ask them where they are going, but you no longer control where they actually do go for the evening. They have the keys and hold the steering wheel in their hands. Power!

Giving up power by giving them power is always risky and sometimes frightening, but we have to allow them such freedom in order for them to grow in areas of decision-making, integrity, and responsibility. A part of growing up, of becoming who you are, comes only when the puppet strings are cut.

God, for many of the same reasons we parents do, offers us the freedom to make choices that include our mistakes. A social God has to give us a choice as that is the only way interaction with integrity can take place. Our children may eat of the forbidden fruit—that is, go where they are not supposed to go in their new freedom. As God's children, we have the same options. We, like our children, are constantly akin to Adam and Eve. That is, we often make decisions not within God's intended will for our lives.

Why doesn't God stop us? Because life would have no value for God or humanity if we were mere puppets. We must choose freely if our choices are to have meaning. Think about it, not even judgment would make sense or have value if God held the strings and we were mere puppets under God's control. If we do not have freedom to choose, then how can God hold us responsible for our behavior?

The same logic spills over into the other choices we make. For instance, we must be able to love freely if love is to have significance. Of what meaning is love if it is not of our own free choosing? Neither we nor God could find value in a puppet love not freely given within and of our own consciousness.

When we come to understand that God has given up some of God's power so that our lives can have integrity and value, only then can we come to grips with the depth of God's communal nature. We are in community together. Just as when our children disobey and disappoint us, and we have to respond to their negative behavior, God has to take into account our responses also.

Therefore, we must never view God as some stagnant monarch seated upon a throne, having dictated the way life is to be. God is, in fact, active, caring, and involved in our daily activities. God is always responding to the choices we make that determine our behavior.

And yet so many folks across the years have told me they find the God of the Old Testament ruthless and uncaring. How misguided they are. Just study (not simply read) the incredible eleventh chapter of Hosea. It is gut wrenching to empathize with the struggle of God as the Eternal One deals with the likes of us. Listen to the loving Father as the Lord experiences our waywardness.

> When Israel was a child, I loved him,
> and out of Egypt I called my son.
> The more I called them,
> the more they went from me;
> they kept sacrificing to the Baals,
> and burning incense to idols.
>
> Yet it was I who taught Ephraim to walk,
> I took them up in my arms;
> but they did not know that I healed them.
> I led them with cords of compassion,
> with the bands of love,
> and I became to them as one
> who eases the yoke on their jaws,
> and I bent down to them and fed them.
> Hosea 11:1-4 RSV

In these four verses we find the great Parent filled with concern, calling us, teaching us to walk, holding us with arms of gentleness, healing us with cords of compassion and with bands of love. I bent down to feed them—us. And now digest our response to our Lord. It is verse number two that we to ingest. "The more I called them, the more they went from me." Who among us, as parents has not experienced the same? We did our best only to see a son or daughter turn away, go astray . . . break our hearts, and yes, cause us to respond angrily.

Incredibly, God was/is experiencing just that! Listen to an angry God.

> *They shall return to the land of Egypt,*
> *and Assyria shall be their king,*
> *because they have refused to return to me.*
> *The sword shall rage against their cities,*
> *consume the bars of their gates,*
> *and devour them in their fortresses.*
> *My people are bent on turning away from*
> *me;*
> *so they are appointed to the yoke,*
> *and none shall remove it.*
> Hosea 11: 5-7 RSV

But God is a bigger SAP than you and me! Listen to the love of our God!

> *How can I give you up, O Ephraim!*
> *How can I hand you over, O Israel!*
> *How can I make you like Admah!*

How can I make you like Zeboiim!
My heart recoils within me,
my compassion grows warm and tender.
I will not execute my fierce anger,
I will not again destroy Ephraim;
for I am God and not mortal,
the Holy One in your midst,
and I will not come to destroy in wrath.
Hosea 11: 8-9 NRSV

Never see the Old Testament God as uncaring or unconcerned. The New Testament Jesus simply is God with skin on . . . The Incarnate One who calls us "His little children." And like the God of Hosea, Jesus calls on us to come to Him. Will you? You're not on a dead end street. It's a super highway!

How is God? There is nothing more positive or significant to share about God than the fact that God will give you and me another chance. That view is based on both the Old Testament and the New Testament's sharing. Those accounts square with my own experiences with God!

Consider again the scripture, this time from the New Testament. You will recall the woman caught in the very act of adultery. Can you imagine her humiliation? Not only was she caught in the act of a great sin, but she was actually dragged into the streets before the community to be used again in setting a trap for the Lord. (John 8:2-11) Everyone knew the law which stated that she was to be stoned to death. (Leviticus 20:10) She must have felt not only humiliation but naked hopelessness.

"What do you say, Jesus; do we stone her?" Every eye was on Jesus. When we read that scripture, it comes alive for us. Feel the penetrating eyes of Jesus as He searches the crowd. There was no answer for what seemed an eternity, and then suddenly the face of God is revealed for all to see. "Let he who has not sinned, cast the first stone." What else could the accusers do, but drop their stones and slowly walk away? There is more going on, however, than Jesus winning another verbal confrontation with the Pharisees. The very nature of God is being revealed; the curtain is being split apart in the temple. (Luke 23:45) Now there is only Jesus and the adulterous woman. Face to face with the Lord of life, she must have wondered what would happen to her now. Looking on her with love's compassion, He asks, "Woman, who condemns you now?" She responds, "Nobody, my Lord, nobody."

"Neither do I; *go* and sin no more." Can you imagine how wonderful that little word "*go*" must have sounded to a woman faced with certain death by mandate of the almighty law?

"*Go*" for you have another chance at life. "*Go*" and get it right this time around. Jesus is offering her another chance. Just when life had never looked so bleak, she suddenly is free to "*go*" again. Grace is the name of that street.

It is important to note that neither Jewish law nor community expectations kept Christ from offering the woman another chance. I have not found the Lord any different in my own experiences with Him. Some years ago I went through a particularly difficult time as a Christian minister. Though many have experienced divorce that statistic offers no help to the individual in the process. As I went through mine, I often felt guilty, alone, professionally marginal, and unworthy of remaining a Christian minister. A number of times I thought about handing in my ordination papers. However, the United Methodist Church appointed me to a church (where I remained for six years) and the Lord said, "Go." I am glad I did! A caution is needed here. The "going" is freely offered, but it is not free. I mean by that we are to go and "sin no more." We go with such responsibilities innate in the Lord's grace.

So what kind of a God is this God who has to do with us? God is the Lord who has given us life of a relational nature, the integrity to make choices even at God's expense, and the chance to recover when we sin or make the wrong choices. How can anyone reject a God like this?

Years ago my son, Brian, went with me to my office located on the second floor of a sizable bank. There was a double lock on the door and, though

I did not realize it at the time, I had locked myself in the building. When I tried to leave the building an hour later, I discovered what I had done and somewhat panicked at my predicament. Edgy and upset, I said, "Son, what on earth are we going to do now?"

Sensing my anxiety, he responded, "Dad, it's all right. I'm not afraid to be in here as long as you are with me." I just picked him up, held him in my arms, and wept. More than thirty years later, I feel somewhat like Brian did years ago. Being here on earth is all right as long as the Eternal One is here with us.

"And they came to Bethsaida. And some people brought to him a blind man, and begged him to touch him. And he took the blind man by the hand, And led him out of the village; and when he had spit on his eyes and laid hands upon him, he asked him, 'Do you see anything?' And he looked up and said, 'I see men; but they look like trees, walking.' Then again he laid his hands upon his eyes; and he looked intently and was restored, and saw everything clearly."
Mark 8:22-25 RSV

Chapter 3

A Warning Light

I play tennis at Palmetto Dunes on Hilton Head Island. After you turn off the main highway onto the road that leads to the tennis center you are on a beautiful stretch of road about a mile long. The live oaks stretch out their welcoming arms all along the way. The speed limit is 25 mph which is perfect unless you are rushing to get to the courts on time. Often they have an electric sign that records your speed as you approach it. If the light flashes on and off, you are going too fast. It informs you that you are breaking the law. At 30 mph it flashes. At 28 mph it flashes . . . at 26 mph it flashes until you get down to 25mph or below. To put it in its theological context it flashes until you get in a right relationship with the law. We can only wish all of life were that way. That there was a warning light that flashes whenever we are not in a right relationship with the Lord. That it would keep flashing until we got it right.

Now, if we ignore the warning light often enough you can imagine another flashing light atop a trooper's automobile. It's then not about a warning. It's ticket time . . . judgment day has come. Why? Because we get caught up in getting to our destination without regard for the rules.

Never forget this. Our sins are generative. *"They have children."* Breaking the speed law generates wrecks; wrecks can lead to injury or death. Small sins can lead to large consequences. There are spiritual signs that we ignore too.

We must let the stories of the Bible speak to us. If the church had a better understanding of them, we would have more insight about our own spiritual blindness and perhaps become more open to God's leading. Without this openness to the Creator, we creatures can remain spiritually blind for long periods of time.

Both the Old and New Testament refer to our spiritual blindness. Consider one of our favorite Old Testament stories. You will find it in the twenty-second chapter of the seldom-read book of Numbers. It's the story of Balaam's ass. What a masterpiece of psychology and theology woven together long ago under God's inspiration! Journey with me to discover the core of its message.

Israel had just overcome the Amorites and were now encamped on the plains of Moab beyond the Jordan at Jericho. Balak, king of Moab, was greatly concerned; frantic would be more precise. Considering Israel's success against the Amorites, he doubted his country's ability to resist Israel in a military confrontation. Balak was looking for another way out; a magic wand would do. Somehow perched on his ear was the name of a diviner called Balaam. His home was in Pethar, a town apparently located on the upper Euphrates River. Mesopotamia was famous for divination, and Balaam may have been one of the better known diviners. How else can we explain how he was known to Balak in Moab?

Balak sent for him with gifts of enticement to make sure he would come. The Lord God apparently did not want Balaam to go (see Numbers 22:22), but he agrees to the journey after some internal conflict and struggle. (Here the story is somewhat jumbled as the author includes two strands of tradition that can leave the Bible reader confused). Our interest in the story begins as Balaam set out on his journey, riding on his faithful jackass. God's anger is kindled against Balaam as he begins his trip and God sets before him an angel with a drawn sword, hoping that Balaam will see the angel and turn back. In this fascinating tale, the donkey sees what Balaam cannot see—the angel of the Lord with sword gleaming in the sunlight. The animal reacts by running off the path and into a field.

Balaam, upset by the animal's unaccustomed behavior, strikes the ass and turns him back onto the path. A distance down the road Balaam continues to ride the donkey, moving between two walls in a vineyard. The scene is repeated with God's angel standing before them. The sword is still glimmering reflecting the sun's light.

Still, Balaam does not see the angel of death sent by God to turn him back. But the donkey sees and, in attempting to get by the angel, scrapes against the wall painfully crushing Balaam's foot between his body and the wall. I love this scene! Imagine Balaam's anger as his foot is mashed between the wall and the frightened donkey's side. Balaam shrieks in agony and strikes the donkey a second time! Injured or not the journey must continue! So still further down the pathway, in an even more narrow place, God approaches Balaam through the same angel.

Once again, the ass sees the angel with drawn sword. The place was too narrow to turn; there was nothing to do but simply lie down. That's exactly what that jackass did! Balaam was infuriated, and he struck the donkey with his staff. Here the story begins to unfold like water rushing to find its level.

"What have I done to you, that you have struck me these three times?" the bewildered ass asks of his master. Quickly Balaam responds with righteous indignation, "You have made sport of me. I wish I had a sword in my hand, for then I would kill you." Not one of us can question Balaam's blind anger. In spite of that, however, the donkey pursues his point. "Am I not your ass, upon which you have ridden all your life long to this day? Was I ever accustomed to do so to you?" (Numbers 22-28-30 RSV) Balaam rightly affirms the animal's faithfulness.

What is the author trying to say? In the verses that follow, the point becomes crystal clear as God mediates between Balaam and the animal. This is it! Succinctly stated, Balaam was so intent on his own way that he could not see God standing in front of him. *In fact, even a jackass could see with greater spiritual clarity than could Balaam!*

That is the point, and it rings too familiar. Often, at the pressure points of life, we are so intent on our own way that we cannot see God. Balaam's ass might have better spiritual vision than even we contemporaries! If we are to journey with God, we must shake the worldly scales from our eyes and become more spiritually astute.

Do donkeys talk? Is this story historical? Those who read God's word must come to grips with this story being transcendent, beyond earthly history. It is of God. Once we come to focus on the author's message, it can lead us toward a spiritual wholeness that works in this world where we reside.

That is the goal, spiritual wholeness. The first step toward that state of being is to see ourselves in relationship with God. One of life's daily challenges is focusing on God rather than ourselves. It may not always be easy to focus on God, but spiritual wholeness requires constant movement in that direction.

Many people do not focus on God, nor do they wish to see spiritually. There is a story that surfaced some time ago about an old camper who lived in a tent. One night he entered the tent with a bag full of figs. The first thing on his agenda was to light a candle by which to see, and he did so. Pulling up a fruit crate in lieu of a chair, he took one of his figs and broke it open, only to find it full of tiny worms. Disgusted, he threw it out the tent door and proceeded to take the next fig from the bag. That fig was also full of worms and met the same fate as the first. When he reached into the bag a third time, he selected a large healthy looking fig; but as he broke it open and held it to the candle, he found that it, too, was full of tiny worms. Fairly disgusted, he blew out the candle, took out a fourth fig, and ate it in the darkness! Sometimes we choose not to see! The camper decided not to see due to his passion for a fig. He wanted his way no matter what the obvious truth may have been. Adam . . . Eve . . . Balaam . . . the old camper . . . the prodigal . . . you and me . . . we're determined to do it our own way. Oh for a warning sign, an angel or just a jackass to set us straight!

Remember how the prodigal son wanted his way so that he might fulfill the passions and appetites of his life? The Father no longer has to do with my life, he thought. Can we think of a better illustration of spiritual blindness and emptiness than this parable of Luke 15: 11-24. The wayward son chose not to see life in relationship with his Father. We, likewise, can choose not to see life in relationship with our Lord. That choice, however, might not be a conscious choice to reject God, but rather the unconscious following of a hedonistic path of self-fulfillment. Ask the prodigal!

Because Paul knew firsthand about seeking the wrong pathways, he could write about the frailty of his and our fleshness. Absorb his frustration as he wrote, "I do not understand my own actions. For I do not do what I want, but I do the very thing I hate." (Romans 7:15 RSV) You and I could have written that! It is sacred scripture, you can be sure, for it is universally our story. We do incredibly foolish things without ever meaning to reject God. Our value system might be acted out as "I'd rather have fun than be right," with no conscious intellectual choice ever being made to ignore God.

Paul's assertion that we can't get it right even when we are trying with all our might points us toward the great need to intentionally focus on God. One reality that we must have noticed about ourselves is that we easily stray. For instance, *generally* speaking, if you were asked to choose between good behavior or bad, you would choose to be a person exemplifying good behavior. However, *specifically*, we often find ourselves choosing to do that which we know is not right or good. Why? Because when we speak of our ideals and desires to do that which is good, we for that moment are not pressed by the factors of life. We're just thinking about how we would like to be and how we believe God would have us be. Choosing to generally be good is easy! However, out in the real world of specific occasions, we come face to face with lust, greed, pride, popularity, and our internal conflicts and desires. Our fleshness, the sin that dwells within, rears its ugly head, and we choose specifically to do that which is wrong. We know better, but we don't do better.

Reflect back on the original story of this chapter's beginning. Balaam faced life with all its pressures. The psychology innate in the story when Balak sends gifts to entice an affirmative response from Balaam is evident. Individual greed often motivates people. In Balaam's case he made the trip to Moab knowing that God wanted him to stay put in Pethar. Why? Because he couldn't refuse the very present rewards that Balak dangled before him. He wanted life's "toys!"

Peter often had Balaam's disease. That's my new name for spiritual blindness. On the lead in page of this chapter I introduced you to a difficult two-part healing of an unnamed blind man. It is a story found only in Mark's Gospel, and it is also the only two-part healing recorded in the Gospels. Further, I am convinced that its insertion in Mark's Gospel is to introduce us to Peter's spiritual ineptitude—his suffering of Balaam's disease.

This is how it goes. Jesus and the disciples were headed toward the village of Caesarea Phillippi, and on the way He engages the disciples in conversation. "You are around the townspeople; what are they saying about me . . . who do they think I am?" (Mark 8:27-30 RSV) Immediately they responded with what they were hearing.

"Some think you are John the Baptist; some wonder if you're not Elijah or one of the other prophets." There is silence for a moment. They walk a little further. Jesus stops. The disciples gather about Him as they sense the importance of the next question. "But who do you say that I am?" There is no silence this time as Peter ushers in a new era. "You are the Christ." But could he see what being "the Christ" meant?

Why do I take this position? Because of the two-part healing! The blind man, after the first touch of Christ can see, but people look like trees walking. Peter can see that Jesus is the Christ, but he doesn't understand what that means. Spiritually, he cannot see with clarity yet. For him and other Jews, the Messiah would come to lead a Jewish revolution. But they were wrong again!

That is why the next scene has such emotional depth, for instead of the Christ being a military revolutionist Jesus speaks of His suffering, rejection, and death. I am intrigued at how Mark wrote it. "And he said this plainly." (Mark 8:32a RSV) No matter how many times I read it, I am never ready for Peter's reaction. Mark sometimes records events with such awesome simplicity. "And Peter took Him, and began to rebuke Him." (Mark 8:32b RSV) Peter grabbing our Savior by His shoulders? Why? People still look like trees walking to Peter. He does not see clearly. He needs the second touch, the second part of the two-part healing so that he, too, can see with spiritual clarity. The point is that Peter was as blind as the blind man brought to Jesus in the preceding paragraph. (Mark 8:22-26) Even as blind as Balaam! He could not see what being the Messiah meant. Suffering and the cross were not visible to Peter. Can the church see?

Balaam and Peter both had their own agenda. Our agendas often blind us! Spiritual wholeness, sight that leads to spiritual insight, comes only when we try to discover God's agenda and purpose for our lives. Neither Balaam nor Peter is unique. We all suffer too much from forming the human agenda. I want a boat, new car, power, popularity and prestige. All the while the "rest of the story" awaits its reading. "If any want to become my followers, let them deny themselves and take up their cross and follow me.

For those who want to save their life will lose it, and those who lose their life for my sake, and for the sake of the gospel will save it. For what will it profit them to gain the whole world and forfeit their life?" (Mark 8:34-36 NRSV)

Now, you and I can be sure that this is the depth of the Gospel. If any mortal would follow Jesus this must be his or her agenda. Denial of self, taking up the cross of Christ, and following Jesus Christ down pathways that "brings" God to everybody. That's it! So simple but can you do it?

I have said so many times to so many people that being a "faither" is not easy for me. Faithing is constantly, almost without exception, hard work. I think the reason begins with self-emptying. Emptying myself of all things that point toward me. I have always admired John the Baptist's testimony in John's Gospel. (1:19ff RSV) Under questioning and in the limelight John flatly stated, "I am not the Christ." "Are you Elijah?" He said, "I am not." "Are you a prophet?" John said, "No."

Then who are you? We've been sent to find out. You baptize, you must be spiritually significant. They could see through John that something was on the horizon. And then John steps up to the plate and swings mightily for God. He points to Jesus and says, "Behold, the Lamb of God who takes away the sins of the world. He ranks before me and baptizes with the Holy Spirit. I have seen and borne witness that this is the Son of God." (John 1:34 RSV) John pointed away from himself so he could point to our Lord. John abandons himself but not Jesus!

You see, John is a better follower than the church. Too often we point to ourselves. I confess to such smallness, to such puny frailty. Too often I consider myself first. Self-emptying is a hard act to follow. Again, John abandoned self-importance.

Again we must refer to Paul as he describes us so well; "I do not understand my own actions. For I do not do what I want, but I do the very thing I hate. Now if I do what I do not want, I agree that the law is good. So then it is no longer I that do it but sin which dwells within me. For I know that nothing good dwells within me, that is, in my flesh. I can will what is right, but I cannot do it. For I do not do the good I want, but the evil I do not want is what I do. Now if I do what I do not want it is no longer I that do it, but the sin which dwells within me."(Romans 7:15-19 RSV)

Later, this agonized soul says he is "captive to the law of sin which dwells within. Wretched man that I am! Who will deliver me from this body of death?" (Romans 7:23-24 RSV)

Paul writes that he cannot get out of his own way, that he cannot empty himself of self. Remember Paul is the author of much of the New Testament and is often described as Christianity's greatest missionary.

Again, he wrote it, but we could have. We often feel his futility, don't we?

Wretched people that we are, who will deliver us from this body of death? More than any other question this one must be dealt with in depth. And John points all of us towards the Lamb of God. It's like this, follow Jesus long enough and your wretchedness will diminish. Why? Because if one looks at Jesus, one sees God. (John 14:9) Seeing God is a humbling experience. The apostles bore witness to such when in Jesus, in His life, death and resurrection, they experienced God at work. Jesus was more than just a man; here was a "window" in which to see God at work. "God was in Christ, reconciling the world to God's very self." (2Cor 5:19 RSV)

Look through that window and you will see what Job saw when confronted by God in Job's great 42nd chapter. "I know that thou canst do all things and that no purpose of thine can be thwarted. I had heard of thee by the hearing of my ear, but now my eye sees thee; therefore I despise myself and repent in dust and ashes." (Job 42: 2,5-6 RSV)

Seeing God through the window of Jesus will do that to you. We discover the creature in ourselves over and against the Creator, God.

In truth, it is not easy to see with spiritual eyes as the world we experience is quite hedonistic. Sacrifice and servant-hood are not often perceived in our noisy selfish habitat. Yet, there is a crying out from creation for us to see. "We know that the whole creation has been groaning in travail together until now; and not only the creation, but we ourselves, who have the first fruits of the Spirit, groan inwardly as we wait for adoption as sons, the redemption of our bodies." (Romans 8:22-23 RSV)

All of the Gospel of John asks that question. Can we see? Well Nicodemus couldn't, (John 3) the woman at the well couldn't see (John 4), everyone in John's ninth chapter was blind, Mary and Martha were in the dark in John 11, and in John's great 20th chapter Mary thought Jesus was just the gardener. They stumbled in the darkness of needs, doubts, preconceived ideas, keeping up with others. Balaam's Disease, the Nicodemus epidemic. So blind. Let's see!!!

"Bread is made for laughter,
And wine gladdens life,
And money answers everything."
Ecclesiastes 10:19 RSV

Chapter 4

Mistakes We Make

here are too many gods in our lives. It is amazing how many arenas there are in life in which we worship. The many gods abiding all around cause us to become fragmented. We want to have the best that each god offers. We are aware that there is one true God; however the secular gods seem so real; they keep calling. Do you ever hear their ranting?

James Fowler authored a powerful book entitled *Stages of Faith* in which he describes people who have what he labeled a "polytheistic faith."5 (p 19) These people cannot commit themselves to one value center. They have a loyalty toward many gods and spend their energies paying allegiance to all of them.

Actually, we put our faith in so many things. We have to in order to live. Persons, causes, institutions, and concepts all call us into a faith relationship. A check on how we spend our energies, what captures our time, what goals, dreams, and visions we have, reflects our centers of faith and value. Where does God fit among the gods? What is your faith center? Do you spend most of your time and energies among the gods rather than with God? Every time our spiritual well runs dry, we are forced to locate and identify the gods who have drained us, who have distracted us from our monotheistic faith and belief in God through Jesus Christ.

Who are these gods who fragment and disrupt our faith center? They are legion! Power, prestige, materialism, popularity, politics, pleasure, and success are among their many names. We spend so much time in their temples. Often I see you there.

One of the New Testament's great tragedies which illustrates our fragmentation and allegiance to other gods is recorded in all three synoptic Gospels. (Matthew 19:16-30; Mark 10:17-31; Luke 18:18-30) The whole matter of one's faith center was surely the focus of the narrative of Jesus and the rich ruler. Remember his question to Jesus? "What must I do to be saved?" And Jesus responded, "You know the commandments: 'Do not commit adultery, Do not kill, Do not steal, Do not bear false witness, Honor your father and mother.'" (RSV) The ruler quickly affirms he has followed the commandments since boyhood. Jesus, sensing that which kept this man of leadership fragmented and without a sense of spiritual wholeness, responds, "One thing you still lack. Sell all that you have and distribute to the poor, and you will have treasure in heaven; and come, follow me." (RSV) Mark records with simplistic power, "At that saying his countenance fell, and he went away sorrowful; for he had great possessions." (RSV) We feel sorry for him. Why? It takes faith to believe in God to the point of placing your sole trust in God—to trust God with your great possessions. You can empathize with the man of wealth, can't you?

Would you have followed Jesus' instruction and given up everything that you had worked to accomplish? Few of us would have been different than the rich ruler. There is great security and power in wealth. We become a little like god and develop an understanding of ourselves to be somewhat superior and independent. A sense of self-reliance forms within our core. It is hard to follow God after the mentality of self-reliance has taken root in the psyche. Succinctly stated, the rich ruler couldn't sell all he had and give it to the needy because he had a different value and faith center than that to which Jesus was calling him. The truth remains, however, we can have only one master. (Matthew 6:24) We must give up the gods to truly experience God.

Emptiness had beset the ruler, or he would never have come to Jesus. That's our identity with this tradition of scripture. We, like the ruler, often feel too fragmented, empty, and spiritually incomplete. It is easy for us to get into his pilgrimage, his skin. We would have approached that Rabbi from Nazareth ourselves and asked, "What must I do to be saved?" And just like the rich ruler we would have hoped that the answer would be easier, less demanding. But it never can be.

Many years ago I was told a story that probably has no historical foundation, but innate within the story is a measure of truth that merits retelling. The story is about a man who for many years had sought God. He went to one spiritual leader after another, but none were able to help him through the spiritual emptiness that marked his life. Finally, he sought assistance from a wise Buddha who agreed to help him.

"Come back tomorrow," the Buddha instructed, "and I will start you on your spiritual journey toward finding God." The next day the man came begrudgingly, at the appointed hour, to meet with the Buddha. "Come follow me," came the soft instruction. The man did so, following the Buddha as he waded into a muddy river. When they were chest high in water, the religious leader suddenly turned and asked, "So you want to find God?" Before the spiritually tormented man could respond, the Buddha had his head under water, holding him there. At first the man obliged, but soon he needed air. Still the spiritual guru would not let him up to breathe.

Momentarily, the spiritual pilgrim began thrashing and thrusting with all his might in his desperation for air. Finally, the Buddha let him up. Gasping for air and trying to cough up swallowed water, the man was enraged. "What is the meaning of what you have done?" he demanded. Without apology the Buddha responded, "When you want God as badly as you wanted air a moment ago, you will find the Eternal One."

The story has a profundity about it. Among the gods, how badly do you want God? For many years I did not seek God. I had a wealth of knowledge, but neither the wisdom nor depth to understand or apply it toward the Christian pilgrimage. I struggled from outside the orthodox circle of faith for more than a decade. That time span began in my early twenties and ended when I was about thirty-two years old. I do not think I prayed once during those years. I was smug and thought too highly of myself. As often happens when we think we captain our ship, the bottom fell out. I was submerged in a sea of bills and domestic problems that left me as directionless as a deck hand.

Single and separated from my young children, I knew I could not stand alone. Friends invited me to their homes, others took me out to fine restaurants, but always the walls seemed to close in and take away my breath. Life was a living hell. Slowly and painfully, I realized the awful mistake. I had excluded God from my life. Now I would retrieve that long ago and almost forgotten relationship that I once had. But I couldn't make contact; I could not pray with sincerity. The relationship had dissipated. God seemed dead, and I was dying. It was a spiritual nightmare.

Often I would sit and intellectualize about God. Could there be a personal God in this world of chaos and disruption? I must confess all of my thinking led me only to deeper despair. My mind couldn't grasp God. I wondered then if I could ever experience the Lord again.

Earlier, in the introduction of this book, I shared how I came to experience God through nature to the point of being able to pray again. Certainly that was an important first step toward spiritual wholeness, but I was to learn it was only the beginning. Contact with God again only whetted my need for a deeper relationship and revelation.

However, I was somewhat like my youngest daughter, Elizabeth, who wanted to go visit Snow Bear in one of our local department stores some years ago. She kept after me until we set out to find the great white phenomena. We searched the store high and low, but no Snow Bear. She was clearly disappointed. Finally, I spotted him! "Elizabeth, come here quickly. There he is!"

I expected her to run up to the friendly white giant, but in awe she clung tightly to me. He was bigger than she had imagined. "Come on," I said excitedly, "we will go together." No amount of coaxing would pry her loose from me. "No, Daddy, let's look at him from here." I was her security, and Snow Bear was too big to trust. "He won't hurt you, Elizabeth; honest. He loves little children and comes to be with them at Christmas time. You can trust him to be gentle and good to you."

She responded, "I know that Daddy, but just let me stay here." Elizabeth never experienced Snow Bear that Christmas. She couldn't let go of her security and trust that gentle snow-white giant. She thought he probably was gentle as I told her he was, but she wasn't able to risk. Think about that; she never experienced Snow Bear.

In that early childhood experience there are great truths for us to discover about our own theological journeys. "No, Daddy, let's look at him from here." How often as I agonized and intellectualized, did I want to "look at God from here." Why? Because it felt like too great a risk to let go of what I thought security to be. I, like Elizabeth, never experienced God as I could have. I heard the messages that God could be trusted, that God had come in Jesus Christ to be with me, that the Lord was gentle and kind. That is, I heard the Gospel and believed it to be true, but I could not quite muster the courage to trust what I had been told. Like my daughter, I protested. "I know that, but just let me stay here." Like the rich ruler of Luke's Gospel I clung to my possessions. And all the while my countenance was falling. But I had met those whose faith was far beyond mine. I wanted to get on that street.

But the secular gods kept ranting. My faith continued in fragmentation, meaning there was no center of solidity that gave me the courage to let go or risk. Life's meaning was elusive and, therefore, often frustrated my attempts to define purpose. Somewhere I had made a great error, a tragic miscalculation, but I knew not where.

I now know what the "great error" was. I was egocentric. I had designed life to fit around me. I was the centerpiece, the focal point, the front and center of everything. Self-importance had been molded like a "golden calf." (Exodus 32:3-4) Idolatry is the name of this street. Think about it—the idol of self. Psychologists call it narcissism! But how do you melt a golden calf named self?

God knew my shortcomings and placed before me that which would puncture my ego, melt the golden calf called self. I will never forget the personal tragedy of another that changed my view of life, showed me the window through which I really saw that which is beyond self and selfishness. It all began like this.

Years ago I pastored a church on the west side of Richmond. There was a little country club in a small community called Rockville. I gave tennis lessons there. Often I gave lessons to a tall, pretty, full-of-life woman named Beverly. She had a husband and two boys who were eight and nine years old. She was only thirty four at the time . . . perhaps in the prime of her life. She wasn't a member of my church but she had membership in my heart.

Her closest friend called me one morning. "Emmett," she said, "they did exploratory surgery on Beverly yesterday . . . and just sewed her back up. There is nothing that can be done and she only has a short time to live. She wants to see you."

I had not known she was ill and, in shock, did not know what to say to her friend. We stumbled through an awkward conversation. The words rattled my psyche. "Beverly only has a short time to live and she wants to see you." Most of me did not want to go but within my innermost self, there was no question that I would go. "She wants to see you." Those words penetrated my idolatry, my narcissism, and buried themselves deep into my soul. Suddenly I felt unimportant.

And I went to see her. I feared the visit. Practiced what not to say! Don't ask her dumb questions like "how do you feel?" I wanted to be careful. My questions were to be "How are you handling this?" And to talk about "setting a goal, like getting home."

I knocked on her door and went in with my skills and fears. I was astonished when I saw her. Her face was pale, but she had the glow of an angel. Before I could speak, she spoke. "Emmett, I'm so glad to see you. I've been worried about you and all the stress you're facing. You're one I've loved so easily." Like Mary of John's wonderful 20th chapter, I'm sure Beverly had seen the Lord! (John 20: 18)

From that visit unto this very day, I have striven mightily to live beyond self . . . to serve others faithfully . . . to offer the best of me to those whom God places within my life. To be retired is nothing. To teach, preach, and serve the Lord is everything! Yes, that visit was eschatological, changed my life completely and forever.**

** I do not intend to imply that Beverly's illness was God's way of leading me out of my own personal wilderness, but rather that good can come from every tragedy.

"Seek the Lord while he may
be found, call upon
Him while he is near; let the
wicked forsake his way,
and the unrighteous man his
thoughts; let him return
to the Lord, that he may have
mercy on him, and to our
God, for he will abundantly
pardon. For my thoughts
are not your thoughts, neither
are your ways my ways,
says the Lord. For as the heavens
are higher than the
earth, so are my ways higher
than your ways and my
thoughts than your thoughts."
Isaiah 55:6-9RSV

Chapter 5

A Cure in the Making

atty and I were drinking a cup filled with euphoria. We had just purchased our dream home filled with skylights and sunshine on beautiful Hilton Head Island.

A manicured fairway rolled majestically behind our new home. A lovely lagoon only added to nature's wondrous scene. Our excitement propelled us toward exploration. The lagoon called out to us and we heeded the call.

A great blue heron glided gracefully past as if it were a personal ambassador inviting us into our new world. The "low country" as this area is known, is full of surprises unlike any place we'd ever lived.

As we gazed across the long smooth lagoon a snake swam with its head and neck above the water. "Look at that snake, Patty," pointing in the direction of its head. I'd never seen a snake swim quite like this one with its head and neck moving back and forth.

Patty doubted it was a snake but being an outdoorsman, I knew it was. I'd seen them many times before in Tidewater, Virginia. My experience trumped her lack of experience. Then its head went beneath the water and the snake came up with a fish in its bill. Within seconds it was on the lagoon's shore tossing the fish in the air so as to catch it head first.

That snake turned out to be an anhinga, a water bird that swims with its body beneath the water and with its head and neck extended beyond the water's surface. Honestly, to save face, the anhinga is often referred to as a "snake bird." This time Patty was right and I was almost wrong.

So often what we know for sure steps up on the shore of life as something quite different.

I've found the Christian journey filled with such surprises. Sometimes we're so sure in our faith journey only to discover a God full of surprises. That's what makes the Christian pilgrimage an adventure pregnant with crossroads.

Many times I've been homeward bound but God called out of nowhere, somewhere, everywhere. Ask Abraham, Sarah, Jonah, Jeremiah, Mary, Elizabeth, Matthew, John, Paul and a host of others.

That's how faithing is. You think you're settled in and God comes. More than perhaps we would like, the Lord is unsettling; confronting us at some crossroads as we travel.

Not all crossroads count for a lot, but some do. Traditional crossroads are at every stage of life. What will I do now that I've graduated? Will I go on to work, or consider a college for additional study? Is this the right person to marry, or should I wait? Should I change jobs at this age? I never thought divorce would infiltrate my marriage; now what will I do? And later in life when a husband or wife has passed away, should I sell the house? Should I remarry? Is anything left for which to live? Crossroads, always crossroads, that challenge and upend us.

Now this is a book about the Christian's pilgrimage toward God, and this chapter is about a "cure in the making." The chapter's theme suggests that something is diseased—that life has a cancer, but good health is still possible! Of course, we are talking here about spiritual health and wholeness. We are now at the crucial point of this book. It is here, at this juncture, that we must clearly understand.

What must we understand? Kenneth Kaufman wrote a poem, entitled "Three Tame Ducks," about the malaise of our faith journey. It is a cancer that we must excise from the Christian pilgrimage.

The poem cites the malady of a "tame old duck" that never flies or adventures beyond the "barnyard muck." On occasion the domesticated duck hears a flock of wild ones flying overhead and senses he is missing something. What's missing ? The very nature of the duck he was created to be.

Suddenly the duck makes a "feeble attempt to fly" and then decides to be "content with the state it's in." One thing is clear; this duck will never fly high in the sky, enjoying the wings of freedom.

Think about that barnyard duck. He stayed so long in the safety of the barnyard that he became grounded! We Christians sometimes seek security, become grounded in our search for the secure places and never attain the joy of one single flight of faith. Faith that is grounded never flies. Grounded faith is an oxymoron.

This is where Kierkegaard's "leap of faith" must become our springboard. Many of us stand on the cliff of life in our ineptness, wondering what would happen if we were to jump in faith. Jump from the springboard of life into the waters of faith! What is its meaning? By this he means to stand on life's edge, as if it were a cliff, and scream, "God, I'm going to trust that You are down there, at the foot of this thing on which I stand ever so precariously. I've tried everything else and have come up empty. I must find out about You because I know too much about me and my ineptness."

Again, it is here that we find our kinship with the prodigal son of Luke's universal fifteenth chapter. How did Luke say it for the prodigal? "He came to himself." And so I repeat it again. "I must find out about You (God) because I know too much about me." Coming to oneself is the humbling realization that you cannot make it alone, that we are inept. The prodigal son went home far wiser than when he left.

Across the years of ministry people have often asked "Why are you a Christian?" I could answer it theologically and point to the incarnation. I'm a Christian because the word became flesh and dwelt among us. God stepped out on planet earth in the person of Jesus. Simple as that! I became a Christian. But that would not be the truth, especially in the beginning when I was faithing on struggle street. I believe, but would somebody help my unbelief!

I could answer, because of the resurrection. God raised Jesus from the dead! After all that was the message of the earliest church's preaching. (Read Acts 2:22, 3:14-15, 4:10) Just read Acts 2:22ff (NRSV), "You that are Israelites, listen to what I have to say: Jesus of Nazareth, a man attested to you by God with deeds of power, wonders, and signs that God did through him among you, as you yourselves know—this man, handed over to you according to the definite plan and foreknowledge of God, you crucified and killed by the hands of those outside the law. But God raised him up, having freed him from death because it was impossible for him to be held in its power." The other scriptures listed above offer the same testimony. That would be a powerful answer and it is the right answer in terms of the reason to believe. But remember, I was laboring, journeying on "struggle" street. Faithing just didn't come easy for me.

Now, I write here, not about experiences that helped lead me to God like the one mentioned in the previous chapter about Beverly. Here I write about my theological struggles. How could I become a believer? What street would lead me to Jesus Christ? Would I ever become a person that could trust God with my life, place my very self in the Lord's hands.

Well, this is partly how I arrived at where I am today. As I constantly study and teach others about our faith I am struck by this fact. Neither God nor Jesus did what I wanted them to do. That's just a fact. Sometimes they still don't.

When I read about Jesus on that wooden cross with nails piercing his wrist and ankles I vicariously feel the pain, a physical hurting. And then when those who passed by "derided him, wagging their heads and saying 'you who would destroy the temple and build it back in three days, save yourself! If you are the Son of God, come down from the cross . . . He trusts in God, let God deliver him now.'" (Matthew 27:39-43 RSV)

And I want it to happen. I want God to take over. I want Jesus to break loose and come down. Show them God! Show them Jesus! Where are the angels? Now is the hour, prime time. But neither ever does what I want them to do. In fact, it gets worse, unbelievably worse. Jesus prays for those . . . those . . . those . . . . "Father, forgive them for they know not what they do." Prays for the enemy . . . prays for those who persecute him . . . who drove the nails . . . who crucified Him . . . executed Him. Read Matthew 5:44 in the Sermon on the Mount.

Well, we become aware of one thing each time we read this scripture. Neither God nor Christ is like us. That's good because if they were like me . . . us . . . then who would we follow? Me? You? Never, for we are very unlike God or Jesus. We first serve ourselves. What we discover finally is this. When Jesus prays, "Father forgive them for they know not what they do," He is praying for me and you! Those wagging their heads, deriding Jesus . . . that's me . . . you . . . out there in the crowd . . . not knowing . . . needing grace. Notice, not just me, you too!!! There is a lot of Herod in us!

Wannabes on the edge of life wondering what would happen if we were to jump. Can I have a faith that dares to trust that much? I jumped! At thirty-five I pushed Herod aside and went back to school (Duke University) to become a minister. I just leaped, saying, "Here I come God," and hoped the Lord would break my fall! God did!

The mistake I made and that you may be making is not to take the "leap of faith." It is necessary if you are to experience the "unsearchable riches" of

God. (Ephesians 3:8) Not to leap is to believe too much in yourself and, therefore, you see too little of God's powerful availability in your life. That is why the account of Zacchaeus, the tax collector, has such intrigue for me. (Luke 19:1-10) Zacchaeus was rich and had job security. Surely he believed in himself. Nevertheless, word was out that the Nazarene Rabbi was passing through town. Apparently much of Jericho was excited about His visit for Luke reports a large crowd gathered. Zacchaeus became curious, but the crowd blocked his vision since he was shorter than most. With great determination and pragmatism, he ran ahead, picked out a sycamore tree which he could climb, and stationed himself in its limbs.

"Ah . . . now I can get a good look at this Jesus," he thought. Peering through the leaves from afar, and with no involvement, seemed safe enough until suddenly Jesus stopped. Perhaps He overheard comments being made about the hated tax collector being up a tree. Just maybe they were calling on Jesus to get their revenge. Who knows how the Lord came to see Zacchaeus crouching in the limbs?

"Zacchaeus, make haste and come down; for I must stay at your house today." Thoughts raced and blood rushed through Zacchaeus' brain. His mind became a "battlefield of conflict." "I thought I was safe up here. How did He see me? Why does Jesus want to stay at my house? What is at stake? What if I don't come down?"

Now, Zacchaeus, will you take the leap of faith or remain "treed?" Zacchaeus became a faither and leaped, placing his trust in the Nazarene. Do not have a mind dulled by stagnation. Let the thoughts penetrate your excited mind and soul. It is a powerful story of transformation after a life riddled with fraud and wickedness. The newly transformed Zacchaeus was now concerned about the poor and those whom he had cheated.

But how can the transformation be so radical? How can repentance have such conclusiveness? Because to take the "leap of faith" means you let go of all you once trusted, all the ways you tried to save yourself, and all of the toys you stockpiled. It is to let go of self as the center of life. You cannot take the leap of faith and hold on to past securities at the same time. The rich ruler mentioned in the preceding chapter illustrates that. You must trust an unknown future to a known God. When this occurs a metamorphosis takes place. As a caterpillar becomes a butterfly you become a new creature. That's metamorphosis street, and like Zacchaeus, we must leap into newness! Rebirth!

To leap you must let go as Zacchaeus did. And when you let go, you understand that you are now trusting God to be God in your life. Life has become an exercise in faith, and you have become a faither.

We must become convinced that all other attempts to be in a relationship with God eventually prove fruitless and futile. Each of us has a choice to make. Will we choose to be like the rich ruler of the synoptic gospels who could not quite trust God to be God, or will we join Zacchaeus in the "leap of faith?" Remember, this is the crucial crossroad's question, and we must not make a mistake at this critical point of the Christian journey. Leap!

But to leap is not enough. Often I wish it were. Spiritual wholeness is a two-part healing as you will remember from chapter three. The "second touch" allows us to understand something of the character and calling of the Lord in whose arms we are now cradled. What the disciples heard in the eighth chapter of Mark, we too must hear. Remember, they took a giant leap of faith when they dropped their nets and tax books to follow Jesus. Few understood their radical departure from settled living. There was no certainty, logic, or reasoning in their sudden exodus from the norm. We must come to understand that those earliest disciples pioneered the primary characteristic of our faith pilgrimage; the willingness to follow Jesus, to take the "leap of faith" from security to adventure.

However, it is not until that eighth chapter of Mark's gospel that Jesus begins the second touch. It is an explosive scene cluttered with raw disappointment and keen frustration. Jesus "teaches" them about the future suffering He must face, about rejection and an impending death. Peter was beside himself and "took" our Lord and rebuked Him. (Mark 8:32) It is apparent that Jesus is not revealing the same course of action that Peter had envisioned. But Jesus knows what has to be done. The intensity of His rebuke of Peter, ("Get behind me, Satan!"—Mark 8:33) and His determination to expound to the "multitude" make it quite obvious that Jesus has determined a clear course for the expression of His Messiahship. *Further, He wants others to join Him.*

Now we must come to understand that the "leap of faith," (stage one of the two-part healing) must be followed by a second touch, a commitment to the very vocational call of Jesus to everyone who dares to claim discipleship. Stage two of the two-part healing has now been revealed. One can scarcely miss the kerygma (heart) of His message. "If any want to become my followers, let them deny themselves and take up their cross and follow me. For those who want to save their life will lose it, and those who lose their life for my sake, and for the sake of the gospel, will save it. For what will it profit them to gain the whole world and forfeit their life? Indeed, what can they give in return for their life? Those who are ashamed of me and of my words in this adulterous and sinful generation, of them the Son of Man will also be ashamed when he comes in the glory of his Father with the holy angels." (Mark 8:34-38 NRSV)

And so, the theological playground of our faith center becomes less cluttered. Jesus has now given each of us a "second" touch. We now know what He is about and what He calls us to be about in this twenty-first century. How will we respond to Him in our time? One does not have to examine the call of Christ over and against the twenty-first century lifestyle with great depth before conflict is apparent. Jesus, on the one hand, is saying that the greatest of us is the servant among us, that to find yourself you must lose yourself in service to others. Our contemporary ethic is in the opposite corner. The most celebrated among us is he or she who finishes number one. Even second place is a sham. Why? Being number one makes all others subservient to me. This is a competitive age of rising stars and monetary rewards.

Which is right, the ethos of Christ or the twenty-first century ethic? For a cure to be in the making, we must choose. We are no longer talking about street names; we must recognize that this is a theological crossroads that can potentially lead us to spiritual wholeness. Who is right? What does it mean to call Jesus *the Christ* and to accept Him as Lord of our lives? How will we respond to the now clear call and vocation Christ has put before us?

There is a story that illustrates this sense of spiritual vocation. A ship at sea was sending distress signals to rescuers on the shoreline that it was taking on water. The call for help was clear as the distressed seamen hoped to be rescued. However, as the would-be rescuers looked at the sea which was growing more tempestuous and the wind which was increasing in its intensity, fear began to play its role. Soon thoughts became words, and a crewman said to the captain, "If we go out there, we may never come back." The grim and fiercely determined captain responded, "We don't have to come back, but we do have to go." His response embodies the spirit of Christ's mandate on our lives.

So, my brothers and sisters, you owe
the flesh nothing! You do not need to
live according to its ways, so abandon its
oppressive regime. For if your life is just
about satisfying the impulses
of your sinful
nature, then prepare to die. But if you
have invited the Spirit to destroy these
selfish desires, you will experience life.
If the Spirit of God is leading you, then
take comfort in knowing you are His
children. You see, you have not received
a spirit that returns you to slavery, so you
have nothing to fear. The Spirit you have
received adopts you and welcomes you
into God's own family.
Romans 8: 12-17, The Voice

Chapter 6

God Never Gives
Up On Us

When beginning this book, I wanted to somehow proclaim the grace of God with vividness akin to the wonder and brilliance of a sunrise spilling over a mountain peak. That goal has not been arrested. This chapter is centered on God and God's marvelous grace. It has to do with all those who have at least glimpsed God at some point in their lives only to turn away. The suspicion is that this is the experience of many. God nudges, reveals, and offers God's self and then watches as the wretched world claims us. We are not really claimed, however; it just feels as if we are. In actuality, we choose to respond to the worldly clamor, the clamor of the gods. Like sheep we nibble our way to lostness. Oh those greener pastures over yonder.

No matter, there are many who were once churched and have turned away, who have heard the "still small voice" (I Kings 19:12) and ignored its message, who have seen the burning bush (Exodus 3:2-5) and kept on their shoes, who have knocked on the door (Matthew 7:7), but only peeked into the kingdom when it was opened. All those times when God had to do with us, and we were not responsive, making our way to Tarshish with an old ancestor named Jonah. (Jonah 1:3)

Perhaps the heart has hardened, and we seldom can hear God's movement among us anymore. Something is almost dead within us now. Spirit. Soul. Purpose. Something beyond the finite. Life goes on, but the death of an infinite mysterium has claimed its meaning. Lameness has taken hold of your soul, and leprosy is the disease of your afflicted life. Still you go on as if life is meant to be this dreadful way. Life is so busy, too busy to search for its meaning. Foolishness is the name of this street. Long ago we forced the Creator's hand in making this street a super highway for its many travelers. Are you one?

Then it happens. A crash on the highway of foolishness. An aneurism of the brain and an athletic son lies in a coma, a mother fails the test of immortality and is claimed by cancer, or a stable marriage crumbles in your lap. Suddenly life is as bleak as a starless night. Just as suddenly life demands meaning. But long ago you neglected, and thereby rejected, God. Perhaps you did not intend to reject, turn away, to choose the world; yet you did. Life's noisy clamor forces your hand. You need God, but can a lame soul go back to the "still small voice," the "burning bush," the gentle nudge? Is God still waiting? Has the Lord's patience endured? Can you go back?

It was an uneventful day until she walked into my office. She was such an attractive young woman, only 39 years old. Her smile was contagious and full of grace. I had no idea why she was stopping by but I was glad to see her. She'd been away from the church for so long she wondered if I'd welcome her back. "Always, you can come back Andrea, always," I happily shared with her.

After a warm embrace I invited her to sit down. She did and then, suddenly her head was in her hands. She looked up with tears streaming down her face.

"Emmett, I'm sick, really sick. Yesterday my doctor told me that I have leukemia. I don't want to die. I'm too young. I'm really scared, Emmett, really scared."

I listened to her share one emotional thought after another. She told me, "I'm going to beat this, I can beat this. Don't you think I can?" After careful reflection I responded, "I don't know, Andrea, I really don't know . . . but I do know one thing for sure. I'll be with you throughout the journey . . . and so will God."

Treatments began very shortly thereafter. As time went on weight loss, weakness and hair loss all became her nightmare. Chemo, plus a bone marrow transplant and every conceivable medical effort was tried. Nothing worked. Her condition deteriorated so quickly that soon she knew that she was not winning the battle, that she couldn't "beat it."

But I noted how strong she became spiritually . . . at times almost upbeat. In the hospital she gave her time and efforts to lift other cancer patients whose illness had progressed further than had hers. Sometimes there is a strength that rises out of weakness. I saw that in her so clearly as she reached out to others.

"Emmett, when it's time to quit fighting this, will you tell me?" I responded, "I'll tell you, *if it were me, when I'd quit.*" One day when she was very weak she asked me if I thought it was time. This is what I told her. "Andrea, the doctors have done all they can do, your friends have been brave and stood by you. The church has been faithful in her intercessory prayers and your preacher has done all he knows to do. But I want to tell you something. It's not over. *God can do what we cannot do. The Lord can go where we cannot go.* That's why we read in John 14, "I go to prepare a place for you, that where I go you may go also."

I put my head on her hand just wanting to bond with her in her fear of the inevitable death she faced. To be with her as much as I could. Apparently she felt my pain. "It's alright, Emmett, God will take care of me. He can do what we couldn't. He can go where we can't." About two weeks later I held her hand and rubbed her head as she passed over to the other side. "You're doing a good job, baby, let go and let God" I said tearfully with most of her family surrounding us. She passed over so peacefully to where we can't go . . . yet.

Obviously, this chapter is going to center on God. It is not meant as a continuation of the human journey or our continued effort to reach God. Instead its intent is to reveal the grace of a God who has infinite patience with the human family. In an electronic age of charlatan preachers and evangelistic entertainment, testimonies have lost their place in the contemporary world. I'm going to give a testimony anyway. *God never gave up on me!* That's it; God never gave up on me. I wish it were possible to convey the deep well of emotion I feel when I offer such a testimony. Often times I was ready to give up on myself and felt others already had, but God never wavered. In the darkest hours of what seemed certain devastation God kept a door ajar or a window cracked through which shone a glimmer of light. You can be certain it was God's lantern of grace. You see, God called me to be a preacher long before I accepted the call. I went in so many directions but that of my calling. Finally, at thirty-five I got it right and enrolled in seminary. It became the greatest leap of faith I'd ever taken!

"God never gave up on me" must be translated into "God never gives up on us." Testimonies are worthless unless they offer universal hope. Search the scriptures, and you will soon discover this great characteristic of God from the beginning.

Moses said, "I stutter" too much to be your man, but God never blinked. "I have Aaron, your brother, to be your spokesman." (See Exodus 4:10-16) And Moses led the Exodus!

Rahab was a harlot, not one that you'd think God would use, but she bravely sheltered two men on the roof of her house who were sent by Joshua to spy on Jericho (Joshua 2:15) plus she is listed in Matthew's genealogy (Matt. 1:5).

David, the youngest son of Jesse, stood before a Philistine giant. He couldn't wear the heavy armor of a soldier nor hurl a man's spear. God gave him a slingshot with which to conquer, and a cowardly Israelite army glimpsed this God of grace. (1 Samuel 17:32-52)

Jeremiah was too young, still God made him a great prophet (Jeremiah 1:6-10.) Peter rebuked and denied Jesus and sank in the sea of life, nevertheless God called him to be the rock upon which the church was built. (Matthew 16:18) Paul was anxious to destroy Christianity, yet God sought him out to become the church's greatest ambassador.

What is the message if not that God never gives up on us! It's not my testimony. It's our testimony—the church's testimony. God has never given up on anyone.

Perhaps though, you have given up on yourself. Your thinking may be such that it seems impossible for God to be in relationship with you. In the preceding chapter I attempted to unfold the cure, the steps needed to truly journey with God; however, you may sense that even in your knowing and taking these steps God would not want to journey with you.

It is time to rid yourself of such thoughts. Join me now as we investigate the journey of another troubled pilgrim named Jacob. He, too, wrestled with God. (Genesis 32:22-32) In these verses you will discover an explosive theological and psychological drama documented through a wrestling match between Jacob and a Stranger. How often God seems the intruding Stranger!

Jacob might have been happy. He had two wives, material wealth, and he was returning home. Nevertheless, in returning home he had to face both who he was and who he had been. Etched in his memory forever was how he had outwitted his trusting old father years ago, and how he had connived to steal his brother's birthright, escaping retaliation by way of a foreign land. (Genesis

27:1-45) He needed to be alone to sift through some of life's debris. For this reason Jacob instructed his family to journey onward while he remained behind. I like how the redactor of this tradition begins the struggle. "Jacob stayed behind, left alone in his distress and doubt. In the twilight of his anguish an unknown man wrestled with him until daybreak." (Genesis 32:24, The Voice) He had been evading the truth long enough. There was something he had to get right before returning to the homeland. The Stranger was confrontive. "You cannot make it right with your brother, Esau, and you cannot out slick life anymore. Now you must face who you really are." They wrestled the whole night through. Note that God does not prevail in the all night struggle. We are free. The Stranger does not strong-arm us. Still you do not come out of this transcendent battle without a limp. God will mark you.

Why recall this ancient tradition of scripture? Because we are to note that though God injures Jacob's thigh, Jacob will not let go of this Stranger. He does not know who the Stranger is ("Tell me, I pray, your name"—Genesis 32:29 RSV), but he knows his life is flooded with darkness.

Now it's daybreak, and Jacob can see that this Stranger is his hope for renewal. Listen to the conversation. "Let me go, for the day is breaking, "says the Stranger. Jacob replies, "I will not let you go, unless you bless me." (Genesis 32:26 RSV) And he holds tight to the shank of God. It is his only chance to get rid of the past. That God allows us to hold on in our plight is grace. That God renames us and invites us back into the fellowship is abundant grace.

The name Jacob means "crafty cheat." Among the ancient Hebrews, one's name identified the character to be expected. It was as if Jacob lived his life to fulfill his name's meaning. He *was* a crafty cheat. Remember how he came into the world grabbing for Esau's heel trying to pull him back in so he could get out first and gain the birthright? And later he tricks his blind old Father to gain Esau's birthright and succeeds! He had even broken his covenant with God when God was not a stranger to him. (Genesis 28:10-22) Certainly he was not worthy of God's continued hope for him; however, God never gave up on Jacob. The Lord never gives up on us. God will never give up on you. God's grace, undeserved love, continuously invites us back into the transcendent fellowship.

How does one survive? Please comprehend this. Life's great wrestling match contains a promise because we are allowed to grab the Stranger's shank and hold on. The Stranger does not shake us off to fall into the abyss of chance. Life and our choices often wound, scar, and maim us, but God will rename us. The Father sent the wounded lamb to heal our brokenness and to offer grace in the most wretched places of our lives. Remember my testimony. God never gave up on me. The Stranger never gives up on us. God will never give up on you. Again, grace is the name of this street.

Why am I so determined to tell you about the grace of God? Preachers often feel most authoritative preaching about God's wrath. Fundamentalism thrives on God's controlling hand throttling your life. I do not buy such theology with the same extremism. Why? Because it is the perceived love of God that molds our journeys best. Fear of God's wrath does not foster creativity, a generative spirit, or loving relationships.

God's love, grace, is the great motivator for holistic living. It was the love of Jesus Christ, undeserved and sacrificial, that changed the world. It was the only power on earth that could unseat Rome. It is the love of God as experienced through Jesus Christ that dethrones us. Nothing changes people into better creatures than when they first perceive that God has loved them all along their journey. A metamorphosis is not just about caterpillars changing into butterflies. It means that a change of character can take place among folks like us. Many have experienced a metamorphosis, a change of mind and purpose.

I remember an ex-convict, we will call him Charlie, speaking to a sophisticated audience about our penal system. He had won the confidence of the system and was a butcher at the penitentiary. Under peer pressure, he began to take meat out of the kitchen to the incarcerated inmates for their consumption. Soon it became apparent that too much meat was missing. Authorities began to search those who worked as butchers. When Charlie came through the door, one of the authorities stopped him. "Charlie," he said, "I know it isn't you, but meat is missing from the meat room, and we're searching everyone who has access to that area."

Charlie recalled that his heart stopped for a moment as he had meat stored everywhere in his clothing. Sweat popped out on his face. The guard began his search. His hands fell across lumps of meat located on his shoulders, in his belt, in every pocket, and even in his socks. Each time the guard's hand fell across a lump of meat, he patted it. Charlie had been caught. "Okay, Charlie, you're clean. I knew you would be." And a stunned Charlie walked back to his cell.

He relayed to us that he was never the same thereafter. The grace of a prison guard changed his whole way of thinking. It was, he related, the first time he had experienced someone being *for* him. That experience of grace remolded his life. Somebody believed in him despite his guilt. It was Charlie's nudge from God, his burning bush, his glimpse into the kingdom, his knowing that God had not given up on him.

This chapter calls us to be reflective rather than reactive, at home in our faith center rather than "all over the place," to root ourselves in the fertile soil of God's grace rather than being restless in the worldly clamor of everyday life. It is a time to center in God's grace rather than be rattled by faithless scattered living.

In earlier chapters I have mentioned the "leap of faith." Kierkegaard coined that phrase in piecing together his brilliant existentialist theology. Permit me to coin another phrase. *Leap back into your faith.* It is important to understand the meaning. When life seems the most burdensome, sometimes we forget the God who said, "I took them up in my arms." (Hosea 11:3 RSV) Spiritual amnesia sets in, and we do not know what to do. We forget to trust in this God of grace who has constantly seen us through crisis after crisis. How can we so easily forget God's leading of our yesterdays? We must leap back into our faith. You can go back!

Paul, Silvanus, and Timothy,
To the church of the
Thessalonians in God the
Father and the Lord
Jesus Christ: Grace to you
and peace. We give
thanks to God always for
you all, constantly
mentioning you in our
prayers, remembering
before our God and Father
your work of faith
and labor of love and
steadfastness of hope in
our Lord Jesus Christ. For
we know, brethren
beloved by God, that he has chosen you."
1 Thessalonians 1:1-4 RSV

Chapter 7

The Church Is
the Answer If . . .

We were walking down the dormitory hall with my arm on his shoulder when he fell dead. He was only 21 years old. We were juniors in college and had been life-long friends. I was to learn later that his faithful and loving parents knew his heart could sustain him for only a few more years, but it was a shocking and sobering event in my young life.

At his death he was only about five feet, four inches tall. He was somewhat hollow-chested and slightly hunch-backed. His eyes struggled in their attempts to focus, and he wore thick-lensed glasses that magnified their weakness. Still he had an infectious smile that made his countenance dance, a quick and witty mind, a determined ethic to do the right, and a love affair with life. To know him meant you quickly forgot his physical limitations. Many loved him.

There is one other thing about him that I will never forget. Each night after we turned out the lights and had been in our respective beds for a while, he would get up and kneel by his bed to pray. He never knew I saw him, but what a testimony that frail praying image was and has been for me down through the years. Like the wounded Lamb of God, there was power in his weakness. He remains a symbol of the church to me.

What symbolizes the church for you? In an age of popular "health and wealth," "name it-claim it," "I want it, God fetch it" theologies, and other heretical "stand-ins" for the church and her Lord, it is an urgent question. What will you embrace as the authentic church of Jesus, the Christ?

Certainly Jesus did not teach health and wealth theology. Instead He called us to be servants, foot-washers, the very least and last, to even deny ourselves in taking up the cross of discipleship. Listen to His words again and again. "If any one of you wants to follow me, you will have to give yourself up to God's plan, take up your cross, and do as I do. For any one of you who wants to be rescued will lose your life, but any one of you who loses your life for my sake and for the sake of this good news will be liberated. Really, what profit is there for you to gain the whole world and lose yourself in the process. (Mark 8:35-36, The Voice)

This isn't "make me happy" theology; instead it is hard-nosed, costly discipleship. One never becomes a follower of Christ in order to receive special treatment or favors. On the contrary, being a Christian in today's world is not necessarily an enviable position in which to be.

Frankly, I'm tired of the church being prostituted (used) from the grass roots to many television preachers. We have all read about the air-conditioned dog house, sexual extravaganzas, and the tremendous personal wealth amassed by many of the electronic beggars who masquerade as ministers. They are obvious to most. What concerns me more is at the grass roots level of the church. As a minister, I'm a veteran. I now know ahead of time when I'm being used. For instance, a young woman introduces herself to me after a Sunday service, flashes a lovely smile, and informs me that she is a member of this church. I'd been the minister there for quite some time, but I had never seen her before. She lived nearby, but just couldn't find the time or stamina to get to church. Three Sundays in a row she showed up. Something's going on! Monday morning the phone rings and, sure enough, it's this young lady. She wants to get married with me as the officiator and in "her" church. After the ceremony, we never saw her or her husband again until a baby was born. The ritual begins again for it is baptism time! Get the picture? The church is being prostituted. Use her when you need her. Worse yet, she does not even have a fee.

Nowadays, if the shoe fits, I ask the couple in premarital counseling sessions if they are prostituting the church. You should see their astonished, offended expressions. I stutter a bit at my own aggression and say, "I mean, why are you getting married in the church? Why is that important? I ask because, until recently, I have never seen you here before." Now it's their turn to stutter. Somehow I gently make my point. At the most important junctures in life people come to the church—to get married, to baptize their children, and to bury their dead. The church is an important institution, so important that you cannot ignore or avoid her. And finally, I ask them, "What does the church symbolize for you?"?

What does it mean to call yourself a Christian? What is the meaning of joining the church? These are important questions upon which all of us must dwell because in order to determine whether the church is the answer for you or not, you must discover *who* the church represents and *what* she actually does. To be sure who the church represents and what the church actually does are not always synonymous. This will always be true as long as mortals make up the membership.

Your investigation needs to focus first on who the church represents. That, of course, is the resurrected Jesus Christ. It has not always been easy for the church to discover who Jesus is and, therefore, what it means to be His bride. I think, however, we have established in two preceding chapters of this book that to be a disciple of Christ is to be uniquely different from the world then and now. We have twice referred to the crucial eighth chapter of Mark's Gospel. What we have discovered is that we must *see* and *do* differently than the community about us. Akin to Peter and his peers, we often have not wanted to hear what Jesus had to say, nor what that difference might be. He calls us to be "towel and basin" people, to play "second fiddle," but it is our human nature to want to play first chair. Someone has said that the symbol that best represents America today is the raised index finger, signifying we are number one. You have seen it time and again on our athletic fields. Athletes proclaim "I am number one" with the index finger held high as the symbolic proclamation.

Even the disciples wanted "first chair" in the kingdom! Remember old Zebedee's sons, James and John? Listen to how they try to set up Jesus. "Teacher, we want you to do for us whatever we ask of you." (Mark 10:35b RSV) How often I have had my children come to me with similar words. "Daddy,

I'm going to ask you a question, but first I want you to say 'yes'."

Ahead of time they want a commitment from me that favors them. James and John were no different. Jesus responds with caution, for he knows our nature, "What do you want me to do for you?" The disciples answered, "Grant us to sit, one at your right hand and one at your left, in your glory." (Mark 10:36-37 RSV) And Jesus talks to them of drinking a bitter cup. Listen to His question of them as if He were asking you. "Are you able to drink the cup that I drink, or to be baptized with the baptism with which I am baptized?" (Mark 10:38b RSV) Afterwards He calls them together to share once again how they are to be as His disciples. Listen to the bitter cup being poured. "You know that those who are supposed to rule over the Gentiles lord it over them, and their great men exercise authority over them. But it shall not be so among you; but whoever would be great among you must be slave of all. For the Son of man also came not to be served but to serve, and to give his life as a ransom for many." (Mark 10:42-45 RSV) This is the Jesus whom the church represents. He came to serve sacrificially, to love sacrificially, and finally, to die sacrificially. He is best identified in the fifth chapter of the Revelation as the wounded Lamb of God.

We wounded Jesus. He healed us. That is a simplistic way of saying His sacrificial journey was to offer healing and salvation to a wounded world, even to those who carved His cross. This Jesus is the Lord of the Church, and we struggle to understand and serve in His name.

Perhaps the best way to gain some insights into Jesus is to follow Him through the pages of an entire Gospel to sense the urgency of His mission, the sensitivity of His character, the radical nature of His baptism, and the frustration He felt because His followers could not comprehend His call from God nor their own sense of vocation as His followers.

It is important to recognize, at this juncture, that Jesus does not operate autonomously. He understands Himself to be an instrument through which the love of God can be best expressed and become functional. He is God's way of offering us forgiveness and reconciliation unto God's self. In short, Jesus, the Christ, is an act of grace. "The Word became flesh and dwelt among us, full of grace and truth; we have beheld his glory, glory as of the only Son from the Father." (John 1:14 RSV) "For God so loved the world that God gave his only Son, that whoever believes in Him should not perish but have eternal life." (John 3:16 RSV)

Now, it is this same Jesus who gives instruction to the church. In the last chapter of Matthew's Gospel we read, "All authority in heaven and on earth has been given to me. Go therefore and make disciples of all nations, baptizing them in the name of the Father and of the Son and of the Holy Spirit, teaching them to observe all that I have commanded you; and lo, I am with you always, to the close of the age." (Matthew 28:18-20 RSV) These are our marching orders, our mandate as the church of Jesus Christ. We are sent forth to evangelize the world, to convert and baptize believers, and to teach them what Jesus has taught us. In Acts, the second chapter, we find the church being empowered by the Holy Spirit to carry out the Gospel mandate. This is *what* the church is about. Both earlier questions of this chapter have been answered in part. We at least know who the church represents and have glimpsed the mission to which she is called.

Now let us go back to the question upon which this chapter is predicated. Is the church the answer for you spiritually as you journey through life?

It is true that some people turn to the church and find nothing. We have churches in every denomination that exist in form, but the spirit is dead. You will not find the celebration of Christ's resurrection or the challenge of His mission within those walls. They exist to maintain themselves. They either have forgotten or have never known the call of the Lord to visit the sick, feed the hungry, clothe the naked, and reconcile the lost. They will maintain themselves awhile longer and then die, for they are not the church.

Others have turned to the church and found rigid codes of morality and little room for grace. The integrity of human freedom to journey with God is not allowed. The authority of the church does not want you to think; rather you are to obey. The faith is externalized into time and place of conversion and codes for appropriate dress. Jesus had more trouble with the law thumpers (Pharisees) of His day than with any other group. These churches need a broader view of the narrow way.

Still others have tried the church and found rituals of mundane predictability and ministers who display very little interest in assisting the congregation in understanding their historic nature. Sadly, these churches have not been led to explore the meaning of their own rituals. Programs and procedures mark their calendars. Are they so highbrow that the meek and lowly cannot find God in their midst?

All of this is to say the church is flawed. We have our problems theologically and pragmatically. The church has painted a picture of a pleasant, easy going, friendly Jesus who belongs to us. But it isn't like that when you read the Gospels.

In the Gospels Jesus is often not close at hand nor understood. I do not believe Jesus is distant just to keep space between Himself and His disciples. The distance is manifested out of the misunderstandings between Jesus and the disciples who thought they were close as followers of the Lord. In truth, they didn't get it; Jesus' ways were not understood by those who were with Him almost daily. Not much has changed.

What we learn is that the longer the disciples traveled with Jesus the less they seemed to grasp Him. Examples are throughout the Gospels as Jesus in frustration asks, "How long must I be with you before you get it?" (Matthew 17:17, Mark 9:19, Luke 9:41, John 14:9 RSV) Luke and Matthew take this particular conversation from Mark, the first Gospel written. The occasion is when an epileptic boy is brought to the disciples by his father and the disciples cannot heal him. After a brief conversation with the father Jesus turns to His disciples and speaks these searing words, "O faithless generation, how long am I to be with you? How long am I to bear with you?"(RSV) And then Jesus heals the boy. Obviously Jesus is at His wits end! In John's Gospel it is a whole other situation that involves Phillip. "Lord, show us the Father, and we shall be satisfied." Jesus responds with frustration again. "Have I been with you so long and yet you do not know me, Phillip?" (John 14:8-10 RSV) Read the rest of the conversation. There are numerous accounts of such misunderstandings in the Gospels between Jesus and His followers. The question remains for the church today. Do we understand Jesus yet?

Even at the betrayal of Jesus, Peter draws a sword to begin a battle and Jesus responds, "He who lives by the sword dies by the sword." (Matthew 26:52 RSV) At the well in John 4 they ask Jesus why in the world He is talking to a Samaritan woman. James and John want the best seat in the Kingdom which doesn't square well with the last may be first. Mary and Martha, thought by many to be the closest to Jesus, don't have a clue who Jesus is when Lazarus dies. Later in John 20, Mary thinks Jesus is dead and that she is talking with a gardener. In a storm the disciples see, not Jesus walking on water, but a ghost!

And the church walks well behind Jesus, just as Peter did in Mark 14:54. There is safety in staying behind. We should ask ourselves today if the church has a better grasp of our Lord. It would be somewhat accurate to say that the church has deserted the Jesus of the Gospels. Read the verse found in Mark 14:51. "And a young man followed Him (Jesus) with nothing but a linen cloth about his body; and they sized him, but he left the linen cloth and ran away naked." I might add, into the night.

What a story! Has the church followed that unnamed young man who was just hanging around. Are we just hanging around? Do we run away naked and into the night when we grapple with who can be ordained or how to deal with homosexuality, clergy divorce and racial injustice? Do we just want to disappear into the night?

We are left with this. Why is the church wearing a robe of royalty and playing games of piety with our storehouses full? Is it our voice we keep hearing, "Dammit, I tell you I do not know Him . . ." Jesus, that is. Naked again. And do you suppose the cock crows and we cannot hear. Or that the Lord looks (as He did at Peter) and we cannot see?

I know I have indicted the church, dug a deep hole from which we must escape.

Yet, do not sell the church short. Think of communities and nations without the Christian Church and ponder what that might mean. The Gospel would eventually be lost, the communication gap between God and humanity would heighten, much of what we consider moral and ethical would lose its base of support, our sense of eschatology (God's control over the final events of human history) would suffer, and a covenant people of God would lose their identity. The human community without the church would be catastrophic.

But let us not dwell on hypothetical catastrophes beyond our scope. Instead I want to affirm the church as I know her, flawed as she may be. What does the church do as a mission arm of God? She proclaims God's healing, sustaining, guiding, and reconciling word; offers the sacraments of the church to God's people; counsels the perplexed in making healthy decisions; visits nursing homes, the hospitalized, home bound, grief-stricken, and lonely people of her communities; offers help to the poor who often come with their hand out; and attempts to evangelize the world. This is only a partial list of the church's ministry; still it is inclusive enough for one outside the church to grasp her mission.

Yes, I was once a critic of the church. I was mistaken. It would be difficult to comprehend my life apart from her now. I have seen the church love, care, reach out, and stretch beyond herself in order to offer Christ to those who hurt. She does because she is His bride. I am a part of her body.

Why do I feel privileged to be a part of this holy covenant community we call the church? Read carefully this unbelievable story. A young, industrious couple were members of my small country church in Chesapeake, Virginia. I was pastor of that little rural church for six years. One night they came to me because they were financially troubled. The husband was a fireman and also a full-time farmer. His life-long dream had been to simply own a farm that would sustain him and his family. They told me that night a startling story of financial disaster. They were more than $200,000 in debt. They could have declared bankruptcy, but they are of the old school; you pay your debts. But how? Like the Israelites of the Exodus experience, there was an army of creditors closing in from the back and an enormous sea of debt before them. Surely they would be devoured by one adversary or the other. (Exodus 14:10-16)

The husband had sold his farm machinery and all but six acres of their land. All they had left was a trailer, the land and a partially-completed house which they were building with their own hands. In thirty days they would lose that also. That night they were not seeking financial help; they simply needed a pastoral ear to bend. Besides, we were close friends.

A few nights later we had a regularly-scheduled board meeting at the church. Someone asked how we might help them. They were $40,000 short of qualifying for a loan large enough to finance their needs. We all agreed it was beyond us. Then some bold soul spoke of nothing being impossible with God's help. (Matthew 19:26) That was theology as Christian as apple pie is American. We set out to try. The great Red Sea was parting. (Exodus 14:21)

The Holy Spirit was moving among us. We were ready to venture into adventure! At the Administrative Board meeting we voted to have our first Good Neighbor Festival designed to raise funds and enjoy the fellowship. Jesus told Nicodemus, "What is born of flesh is flesh, and what is born of the spirit is spirit" (John 3:6 NRSV). This venture was born of the spirit.

The first steps were to organize the festival. Two huge black iron pots were obtained that were used to make chili in one and Brunswick stew in the other. Each pot probably held 25-30 gallons of soup. Picnic tables, banners, and homemade crafts were everywhere. Baskets, jewelry, pottery, bird houses and feeders were sold. In addition, local merchants donated large and small items to raffle through ticket sales.

A lot of money was raised but not nearly the $40,000 needed. But the winds of the spirit were still blowing and local television stations were at the scene to tell the story of our mission. Soon a national news station picked up the story and broadcast it across the country. My son, Brian, who lived in Arkansas, was startled to see me, the family we were helping, and our little country church being featured on a news program. We had made national news! Indeed the waters were being parted. (Exodus 14 RSV).

The next days were so exciting. We had letters from Alaska, California, and Florida coming to our front door. Several of us began counting the money that afternoon. A gift all the way from California to Virginia had to be a large donation. In the envelope was a lovely note and a dollar bill. I looked at one of the church members and said, "It's only a dollar." He shook his head, eyes welling up, and said, "I know, Preacher, but it's worth a thousand." He was right, for within the envelope was the spirit of love, the power that parted the waters and allowed us to help our troubled family cross over to the other side. We wept together.

In three weeks over $45,000 had been established in a fund for the young family. I went with the husband to help get his loan. Nope, nothing is impossible with God. Their home had been saved.

The next month our administrative board met again. The minutes were read, and our expressed doubts had been dutifully recorded. We noted the theology that had pushed us forward. We were in a celebrative mood, for the waters had been parted and we had marched through. We had been the church in mission as Christ mandates.

Is the church the answer? You bet it is! Salvation is the name of this street. Travel on it for, after all, God travels with us!

*In the year that King Uzziah
died, I saw the Lord sitting
on a throne, high and lofty; and
the hem of his robe filled
the temple. Seraphs were in
attendance above him; each
had six wings: with two they
covered their faces, and with
two they covered their feet, and
with two they flew. And
one called to another and said:*

*"Holy, holy, holy is the Lord of hosts;
The whole earth is full of his glory."*

The pivots on the thresholds
shook at the voices of those
who called, and the house filled
with smoke. And I said:
"Woe is me! I am lost, for I am
a man of unclean lips, and
I live among a people of unclean
lips; yet my eyes have
seen the King, the Lord of hosts!"
Then one of the seraphs
flew to me, holding a live coal
that had been taken from the
altar with a pair of tongs. The
seraph touched my mouth
with it and said: "Now that this
has touched your lips, your
guilt has departed and your
sin is blotted out." Then I
heard the voice of the Lord saying,
"Whom shall I send, and
who will go for us?" And I said,
"Here am I; send me!"
Isaiah 6:1-8 RSV

Chapter 8

Find Your Church

e live in an age of the transfers. If you read the church newsletters around the country the new members transferred in from another geographical location or just from another local church. Yes, many transferred in from another local church. Why? Disagreements in theology, church ritual, lay people who squabble while doing ministry together and with the minister for a variety of reasons. In addition, social issues like gay and lesbian ministers being ordained, and the church's many positions on same sex marriages often cause many to leave. Churches grow today because people leave in disagreement and join another church. Not many conversions increase the mainline church rolls!

The church is confronted with so many issues today. That you are the church means that you are confronted with all of those issues too. That's why you need to get straight your theological beliefs before you join a church. Find out the theological position of the church you are attending and how it squares with the teachings of Jesus before you join that particular church. Check out Jesus' position on today's controversial subjects. Not a friend's position, not the most popular position . . . but what is Jesus' directive while sharing with us about the Eternal One.

We generally don't categorize churches other than by denominations which characterize different belief systems. (Baptism is a primary concern for different denominations as to when and how it is to be done). But here I want to divide the church as either pathogenic or salugenic.

By pathogenic I mean those churches that are diseased, suffering from internal conflict and a slow spiritual death. Note in the book of Revelation to John that seven churches are listed and most have pathogenic qualities. Two examples are as follows. In Revelation 2:4 the church in Ephesus has "abandoned the love you had at first." (RSV) Church number seven is Laodicea (3:14) which is "neither cold nor hot." (RSV) The pathology is that she is "lukewarm." (3:16 RSV) Each church from one to seven has a malady, something that is wrong. And by the way, the seven churches represent the church universal! Read about all seven churches beginning with Revelation 2:1 and ending at 3:22.

Note, however that each Church has good qualities also. These are the salugenic qualities that represent that part of the Church that is healthy, a spirituality that is generative and leads people to wholeness and salvation. To be a healthy Church she has to at least know her vocation.

That vocation is trawling! In Mathews County, VA, as a boy, I used to see boats pulling a dragnet (a big bag-like net) behind their boat. My dad use to say to me "They're trawling." It was a way of making a living in my hometown. Fish simply got caught in the net as it was being pulled by the boat. Catching fish by trawling!

Sounds like evangelism to me! Trawling for souls. But does the Church ever trawl? The Church either knows her vocation or not. In this respect she is either salugenic or pathogenic. Not to be pessimistic, but I do not see, within mainline churches, much trawling activity. It's not the persona of very many churches. Yet I read in Matthew 4:19 where Jesus called out to Peter and Andrew, "Follow me and I will make you fish for people." (NRSV)

Now, I want to share a recent conversation I had with a former member of the church that I attend and at which I teach each Lord's day. For the sake of anonymity I'll call him Jim.

I greeted him and said "Good to see you friend; seems a while since I saw you. You okay?" He was glad to share that he "no longer attended 'your' church," as if it were my church." Further he said he had to leave because of the church's position on ordaining gay or lesbian men and women. I listened. He wasn't finished and so on he went. "It was anti-biblical, against the teachings of Jesus, and for sure, against the theology of the Old Testament. The Bible is very clear," he continued.

And so I asked him, "Then the church where you attended and I am still attending is sinful in thoughts and practices?" Quickly he responded, "Absolutely." "We are wrong-headed, sick in our thinking, right?" Again, "Absolutely." I said, "Then, you should still be there, Jim."

"No, no," he assured me. He had to get away from "those people" of which I was one! He then called me a "liberal." *What was he missing?* I'll tell you. Matthew 9:12, Mark 2:17 and Luke 5:30ff among other things. The Synoptic Gospels in unison say the same thing. Let me lift up for you Jesus' teaching from one of the church's Gospels, Luke 5:30-32, The Voice. "What's wrong with you? Why are you eating and drinking with tax collectors and other immoral people?" Jesus answered, "Healthy people don't need a doctor, but sick people do. I haven't come for the pure and upstanding; I've come to call notorious sinners to rethink their lives and turn to God." He was speaking to the scribes and Pharisees. Remember, Jim called me a liberal. I would call him a Pharisee, but I would stand by him hoping to lead him down a more understanding and generative pathway.

Now, let me be clear. I am not saying that lesbians and gays are sick. Nothing in me wants to label another sick for I am sick myself. We are all sick. My point is that Jim should heed the call of Christ; if he thinks his former church is sick, he then should stay and try to heal our ill thoughts and not abandon us. Jesus Christ would never abandon our church! Is Jim a disciple? I must not judge but I hope I have made a point. Don't transfer away from what you think is a sickness. Jesus calls us to be "healers" not an abandoning breed. Someone once shared "He who wishes to secure the good of others has already secured his own." So many want to go where they can be fed. Too few want to go where they can feed. The Church often seems upside down!

So, my point is, as Christ had to work through the meaning of His Messiahship in the wilderness confrontations with the satan after His baptism so do we have to work through what it means to be a disciple of Jesus Christ. Faithing is not an easy road to travel.

Already, and more than once, I've shared in this book that faithing is a difficult journey for me. Read the eschatological Sermon on the Mount (Matt 5:1-7:29) again and be reminded of why. Very little of the Sermon on the Mount appeals to us. It's not our style. It doesn't fit into our culture. It must be outdated—old fashioned—not for this time in our progressive history. It seems too harsh. Let me be very confessional. I don't like Jesus, but I've fallen in love with Him. His teachings are a noble ascent to the top of Mt. Ethics—a holy mountain that beacons out to be climbed. Ever been to the top? Me neither!

Whether Jesus meant to or not He created conflict. Some accepted and followed Him. Some would not follow and openly rejected Him. The conflicted points of view existed even within His family and among His friends. We read in Mark 3:21 (RSV), "When His friends heard it, they went out to seize Him." They continued, "He is beside Himself." In the following verse the scribes, coming from the holy city said, "He is possessed by beelzebul."

A few verses later "His mother and His brothers came; and standing outside they sent to Him and called Him." Then a conflict ensues as to who is His mother and brothers. (Mark 3:31f) And yet many followed and thought He was the Messiah. His works were many and mighty and His followers grew. Constantly crowds gathered awed by the miracles and the authority of His words. And yet there was often conflict. Doug Hare, in his book (p. 15), reminds us to "scoff not at Herod until you have acknowledged the Herod within yourself." 6

So let's look more closely at what Jesus asks of each of us. It isn't so much that Jesus calls us to leave our professions and possessions as it is that we must leave our present understanding of the world behind and enter into a new world understanding. Unless we enter into this new world understanding (rebirth) we cannot follow Him. Ask Nicodemus! (John 3) He just didn't get being born again as a whole new understanding of life.

Listen to this! Our task is to share a faith that is exciting enough to be contagious. (Hare p. 31)6 Pray for the church to find answers that would make the Christian faith more communicable! I really think I know what's missing. Read the following carefully! But it would require going back to the days of Paul the apostle. If the church would begin where he began we could get it done. The church must absorb the following scriptures.

Read them quietly and discover Paul's foundation for evangelizing! In Romans 2:16, Paul writes "on the day when, according to 'my' Gospel, God through Jesus Christ, will judge the secret thoughts of all."(NRSV) In Romans 16:25 (NRSV) Paul continues in his book of books to share, "Now to God who is able to strengthen you according to 'my' Gospel . . . ." And continue to read in 2 Timothy 2:8 (NRSV). "Remember Jesus Christ raised from the dead . . . That is 'my' Gospel for which I suffer hardship even to the point of being chained like a criminal." 7

Please note the most important word in these three scriptures. "My" is the key word. My Gospel,

Paul writes in all three of these scriptures. My Gospel. If ever the church claims the Gospel as hers maybe she could heed her calling found in Matthew 28:19, "Go therefore and make disciples of all nations, baptizing them in the name of the Father, the Son and the Holy Spirit." (NRSV) And then read that final truth left to us! "And remember, I am with you always, to the end of the age."(NRSV) Sounds like evangelism street. Don't transfer away from your calling! It's your Gospel. Mine too!

Transfer? Transfer to where? Another church filled with people who are theologically challenged and don't read the one book that was scripted for them/us. Read carefully now. You shall not kill—no you cannot even be angry with another. Make friends with your accuser while you're going with the accuser to court. Don't lust because that's as bad as adultery. Don't swear for you are not in a position to control what happens. God's in charge of what happens. Forget revenge (eye for an eye, etc.), hitting back for the sake of getting even (revenge is God's business), and go the second mile when forced to go the first, and don't forget to give to him who begs from you. Love your enemies and pray for those who persecute you. From where does such a world view come? Don't worry, it's just the Sermon on the Mount . . . Jesus' ethics. The climb to the top of Mt. Ethics is exhausting. It is exhilarating too! The newness of this Christian ethic is astounding. I've

FIND YOUR CHURCH

always wanted to live bigger than I do. The invitation into beyondness compels my love and devotion to the Lord. He will never let me be just me. Jesus calls us to live above human nature. I love Jesus for moving me toward where I would not go without the spiritual gravitational pull from Him. Sometimes I can join Jesus in saying, "not my will but thy will be done." Sadly, often times I cannot quite get the harmony right. Mt. Ethics is steep!

Ascending the ethical mountain with Jesus is cataclysmic. That is, it changes the structure of whatever street you are travelling. Let me illustrate. Jesus spoke this language once. "This is what our scriptures come to teach; in everything, in every circumstance do to others as you would have them do to you." (The Voice, Matt. 7:12) We call it the Golden Rule. It deserves special attention because it has become so important in Christendom. Clearly it was said numerous times in a whole host of ways before Jesus said it. Tobit, a pre-Christian apocryphal book reads like this. "And what you hate, do not do to anyone." (Tobit 4:15) Hillel, a great contemporary thinker of Jesus' day and a Jewish Rabbi said it only slightly different, but with the same meaning, "What is hateful to you, do not do to your neighbor; that is the whole Torah . . . go and learn from it." As you have read above, Jesus said it positively but with the same meaning. Treat others as you would want to be treated. Douglas Hare notes in his commentary of

Matthew, that there is a difference. "If it is hateful for you to starve, do not act in such a way that your neighbor will starve." If it is said slightly different, "If you wish your neighbor would keep you from starving, you must feed your starving neighbor." The second statement seems to call one into action, (that is, feed your starving neighbor) whereas the first seems to say don't do anything to starve your neighbor. It is more passive and doesn't call one into action to prevent starvation. Which is most like the Golden Rule? 7

But here is the more important point. It is not if it was original with Jesus but whether it is grounded in the Christian genre. For instance, if it is secular then it might be rendered, "Don't report illegal behavior if you don't want anyone to report your illegal behavior." In other words if the Golden Rule is of an anthropocentric genre and points to our activity based upon protection of self, then the rule no longer is golden. What makes the rule golden is if it is interpreted in light of the Christian context of Luke 6:36 which offers, *"Be merciful, just as your Father is merciful."* Specifically, in the Bible, the Golden Rule is to be offered within the Christian context of your interest in others, not self-interest! For a more in depth offering I again refer you to Douglas Hare's book on Matthew in the "Interpretation" series. (Pages 79-81) 6

My point is that the church must understand the theological base for one of her most basic rules or she (we) cannot be the church. With respect to that real life conversation with Jim, he would never have left "his" church had he read the Golden Rule in this way. If I find you sick I will do for you as God would, and if you find me wrong-headed, sick in my thinking, then please do not abandon me but attend to my illness. It would be harder to just transfer to another local church if we understood our own theology.

Why do we live in the day of church transfers? Well, we could begin with the obvious. It's a transient society. We move a lot more than we ever did before. Every time we move, if we are Christians, we look for a new spiritual home. That's one answer for sure. My wife and I did that when we moved to Hilton Head Island eight years ago. It was tough, especially as a retired minister, to find a place where we could feel at home.

In addition, denominations do not matter much anymore. I was a Methodist, Presbyterian or Baptist replaced I am a Methodist, Presbyterian or Baptist. Read that carefully. I *was* instead of I *am*. Loyalty to denominations counts for very little in today's process of choosing a church home. So people transfer from not only one church to another, but also from one denomination to another. In fact, non-denominational churches are the fastest growing churches in America. They are autonomous and people like autonomy . . . freedom, power. We are free to make our own rules, theological positions, and other seemingly important choices. Don't fence me in with denominational regulations is routine thinking today.

And let's be very honest. In mainline denominations we seldom see a conversion experience. Confirmation classes and transfers are how church rolls grow today. Why? Because there is almost a total lack of preaching with a call for repentance. That word means turning from self toward God. Metanoya is the Greek word to ponder here. If becoming a Christian has soteriological (salvation) implications then how can we neglect the call from self toward God? Isn't salvation still the important business of the Church. In fact, isn't this still our first calling? (Matt 28:19) "Go therefore and make disciples of all nations, baptizing them in the name of the Father, and the Son and the Holy Spirit." (RSV)

Prophetic preaching is becoming a lost art. Sermons of conviction concerning our failures within and outside the walls of the Church need addressing. The Church needs to exercise her authority as the bride of Christ. You need to ask only one question to understand the "get along by going along" style of playing Church. Why are we still the most segregated institution in America? Does that issue alone not deserve a prophetic sermon that calls for the church to repent?

When I moved back to Virginia in the mid 1970's I directed the state's first Probation House. One of the leaders on the board to get it started was an African-American educator whose husband was Williamsburg's first African-American doctor. They were a fabulous couple, generative, warm and offering freely of themselves to the community.

In a short time our friendship evolved to the point of sharing stories of our earlier days during this country's racial tensions. Many years ago I had begun doing penance for my race with respect to the days of slavery and also the days when slavery continued even if greatly disguised.

She told me two stories from her earlier life. The first was when she and her husband were driving from New York to Atlanta with their two young daughters who were still drinking milk from a bottle. They stopped several times at restaurants (in that day it was too late for stores to be open) to simply buy milk for their young daughters. No restaurant would let them in! They ended up using coke diluted with water for their children to drink until they got to Atlanta.

The second story was when they settled in Williamsburg. Remember, he was a medical doctor and she was a guidance counselor. She went to buy an automobile and after looking at several cars (she was led to the used and the cheaper cars) she didn't like any that the salesman tried to get her to buy. "Well," the salesman said, "you know what you can afford." They split.

The salesman was told who she was and asked why he wasn't able to make a sale. Realizing his mistake, based on the color of her skin and his perceptions of such, he called her back that afternoon. "Why didn't you tell me who you were? We have beautiful automobiles that you and the good doctor would enjoy." Of course, she was furious. So was I!

Most of us know prejudice at one level but at this everyday mundane level—well I had never imagined how awful that must be. The psychology of penance again flooded my being. It has never subsided over the years and I live among friends everyday who don't know what we have done in the most subtle of ways. They're all churched but what does that have to do with it? The Church hears only a "small" diluted voice concerning prejudice in America. Nothing prophetic. We continue to live at the foot of Mount Ethics. Ready to climb yet?

And stick a fork in evangelism. It's done or done for. Who wants to evangelize today? Why don't we? Because we think our faith is a personal matter. Of course, Jesus never thought of the Christian faith as a personal matter. Over and over pastors have heard "You don't have to go to church to be a Christian."

Well, that is not the theology of the New Testament. In fact, had it been, an institution called the Church would never have happened! Get it straight. We are the Body of Christ! The church is not made up of individuals *who can go their own separate ways.* Togetherness is the heart of the church. We are one body with many talents that must be utilized for the good of the community. Read 1 Corinthians 12:4-26. You must read each verse and make it a part of your spiritual life. To summarize Paul's teachings, the body has many parts—eyes, ears, feet, hands—and each part of the body is dependent upon the other. "There are many parts, yet one body." (1Cor. 12:20 RSV) One of us cannot say to the other, "I have no need of you." Within the Body of Christ we all have need of each other. And our community has need of a church whose many parts operate as one body for the common good.

If we understood our need for one another and our calling to do the most good we can for the community of Christ we would have far fewer transfers. Transfers from afar are necessary and a blessing but we have confused transfers with conversion. I would rejoice to see just one more conversion experience where one soul, empty upon arrival, was filled with the Holy Spirit and publically ready to travel with Christ down Cross Street.

Maybe three years ago our church started an eleven o'clock Sunday School class that began with only 3 or 4 people. The class was entitled "The Exodus: A Journey We All Must Take." I felt rather ill-used in that small class for quite some time. And then it happened! A very attractive middle-aged woman with a fallen countenance made her way up the steps to our classroom. She had a story, but she held her cards very close to her chest.

Surprisingly, before the class was over, she began to deal the deck. She was a leader in the business community in Florida and had her own business which was very successful. She was, as we say, "well-to-do." She and her husband were splitting up. He had filed for divorce. She was a devastated aristocrat, drawn by the title of the Exodus class. She shared she felt she was wandering in a wilderness and wanted out. She needed an exodus experience to exit from her pain. Turns out she needed our small little class of caring people.

Patty and I took her out for lunch after that first class. We both, having experienced her pain, immediately felt a connection with her, and she, with us. The wounded healer concept was at work along with the Holy Spirit.

She kept coming back to class, shared her story with the seven or so people (the class had grown) in that little "upper room" class and soon we all felt free to share our pieces of pain and shame. God had sent her to us, we were there for her, and the real meaning of the Body of Christ became evident as we healed one another's wounds simply by listening and being there for one another.

Every Sunday Patty and I would look for her, walk by and simply pat her on the shoulder and then move on to our seats up front. And do you know what—soon thereafter she joined the church! The Body of Christ was still at work offering love, acceptance and inclusiveness. She never thought of that class as being small. Neither did the Lord. How quickly my concept of "small" changed! When will I ever learn?

Are you seeking a church home . . . your spiritual place in which to worship and reach out to the larger community? Will you seek the church that suits you the most or the church that needs you the most?

Choosing your church home within the community is no easy task, for you have needs too. Christ would not want you to neglect your needs either. I mean, if the needs of others are important, so are yours!

Do you want a church that focuses on fear of hell and seeks conversion based on that fear? Something like 60% or more of Americans believe in hell! You don't meet many folks wanting to go there! So, should you seek a church of evangelical fundamentalism that preaches for conversion based more on fear of eternal fire and brimstone rather than the character and power of love as expressed in Jesus, the Christ?

This we must firmly believe. To hold on to a faith because you seek your salvation, what is best for you, is not Christian; it's selfishness! If you love Jesus simply based on what He can do for you, then you may be in trouble! Read Matthew 25:34-40 for it holds within its words the truth of salvation. "Then the King will say to those to His right, come here, you beloved . . . claim your inheritance . . . you shall be richly rewarded, for when I was hungry you fed me. And when I was thirsty, you gave me something to drink. I was alone as a stranger, and . . . you welcomed me into your homes and into your lives. I was naked and you gave me clothes to wear, I was sick and you tended to my needs; I was in prison, and you comforted me." (The Voice)

And now note the response of those being saved. "Master, when did we find You hungry and give You food? When did we find You thirsty and slake Your thirst? When did we find You a stranger and welcome You in or find You naked and clothe You? When did we find You sick and nurse You to health? When did we visit You when You were in prison? And Jesus responds, "I tell you this: whenever you saw a brother or sister hungry or cold, whatever you did to the least of these, so you did to Me." (Matthew 25:40, The Voice)

In this scene Jesus clearly illustrates for us that to be His disciple one must heed the call to servanthood. In serving the very basic needs of the "least" of our world, we serve Jesus Christ. We do not do this to secure our place with God. We do not do it for the sake of personal salvation. Remember, in this parable the servants did not even know what they had done to deserve entrance into the kingdom. We do it because we have emptied ourselves, let go of self-importance and have allowed Jesus Christ to dwell within us. Remember the leap of faith! Now when we look at our reflection in the pond, it is less appealing. We no longer drive on narcissistic street. The golden calf called self is being melted. Perhaps we can even see something of the image of Christ shimmering back at us. Seeing something of Christ within the reflection of our lives; moving on toward perfection; almost cured! Read the incredible climax of this text. If we are motivated by the Holy Spirit within, then we are in the Lord's eternal grace. Matthew 25:46 reads, "the beloved, the sheep (the righteous) will go into everlasting life." (The Voice)

And finally, you must read the text just before this text. (Matthew 25:41-46a, The Voice) Here you find those who never saw the sick, hungry, naked, homeless or friendless. And, of course, they never lifted a hand to help. Didn't recognize the street they were traveling.

But I do not want to leave you supposing that your salvation is based on works. Paul was clear. You are saved by having faith in Jesus Christ, or as some scholars have interpreted these words in

Romans, you are saved by having faith as Jesus had faith. Either way, we must be faithers and that will lead us into seeking Christ in every person we meet. Salvation is the name of this street.

In much of this book I've mentioned streets we've traveled as if they're clearly marked. As you have just read this is not always the case. This is emphatically indicated in the book of Proverbs as well as the text above in Matthew.

First let me introduce you to two women. One is Lady Wisdom and one is Dame Folly. Let's do a background check on each of them. Lady Wisdom is basically unknown by the Church in terms of her credentials. Check out Proverbs 8:22-32 to learn that God created her as one of the Lord's first acts (8:22). She was established before time, before earth saw its first sunrise. Her claim is she was, existed, before the mountains were placed on their foundation. In reading Chapter 8 we find out she was created before God created the sky, the heavens . . . before the earth was formed. What a lady! Read about her, get to know her, and listen to her instruction.

And then there is Dame Folly. You don't need any introduction to her. Likely you've met her; haven't we all. Read Proverbs, chapter 7:10-22 for a clear introduction. She's clever, up to no good, and she calls out to all who do not know better than to enter her company.

Here is the bad news. Both Lady Wisdom and Dame Folly live on the same street! Life is confusing on this street. You need a spiritual GPS to get the directions right! Read Proverbs 9:1f about Lady Wisdom and her invitation to you and then read 9:13f to receive your invitation from Dame Folly.

Same street. Two invitations and a choice to make. One offers life, the other, death (Proverbs 9:6 & 9:18). The question isn't to whom you are attracted but why. Your destiny is ultimately a matter of choice, not chance. Proceed down the street with caution. Follow your faith in choosing between these two lifestyles being offered.

I've been down the street a ways, not seeking salvation, but to offer salvation. How? By scattering the seeds along the way. Not my seeds mind you, but the seeds that Jesus spoke about in Matthew 13:3. In truth that parable has never been about the four soils. It's about this. The seed is *good seed*. And equally important is that scattering the seed is my vocation and yours too. Jesus calls us to sow the seed everywhere no matter the condition of the soil. Want to join me? It is vocation street and we must get to work!

Notes

1. Soren Kierkegaard, Repetition: *An Essay in Experimental Psychology,* trans. By Walter Lowrie (Princeton: Princeton University Press, 1941).
2. Krista Tippett, *Einstein's God* (New York: Penguin Group, 2010), p.22.
3. James Weldon Johnson, *God's Trombones* (New York: Penguin Books USA, Inc., 1927), pp. 17-20.
4. Paul Tillich, *The Shaking of the Foundations* (New York: C. Scribner's Sons, 1948), p. 60.
5. James W. Fowler, *Stages of Faith* (San Francisco: Harper & Row, 1981), p.19.
6. Douglas R. A. Hare, *Interpretation, A Bible Commentary for Teaching and Preaching, Matthew* (Louisville, John Knox Press, 1993), pp. 15,31,79-81.
7. W. D. Davies, *Invitation to the New Testament* (New York, Doubleday & Company, Anchor Books Edition, 1969), p.22.